VALUE AND OBLIGATION

VALUE AND OBLIGATION

The Foundations of
an Empiricist Ethical Theory

ALEXANDER SESONSKE

A GALAXY BOOK

New York   OXFORD UNIVERSITY PRESS   1964

First published by University of California Press, 1957
First published as a Galaxy Book, 1964
Printed in the United States of America

CONTENTS

Chapter I

INTRODUCTION

IN THE REALM of politics and practical affairs, the twentieth century has thus far been an era of moral conflict and uncertainty. The ideals of peace, progress, and the triumph of reason and decency have been attacked on many fronts and finally shattered by the wave of tyranny and terrorism, war and revolution, which has engulfed us all. Through all this, it has been only the incorrigible humanists who have refused to relinquish the ideal, who have gone on thinking man worth saving and salvation possible. By now, perhaps, their stubbornness has been rewarded as their ideals become restored in common faith. We assent, hopefully, dubiously, to the view that the threatening instrument of our destruction may yet prove the key to the welfare of mankind. But the ideal of progress thus revived cannot be identified with the ideal we abandoned five, ten, or thirty years ago. Our new faith cannot bury or ignore the experiences of these last dark decades. If we believe in progress now, its goal is not a world in which conflict and difficulty have ceased to exist, but a world in which good will and effort may solve the conflicts and surmount the difficulties that will continue to arise. We understand now that an ideal of progress need not demand a goal of perfection, or at least that progress may be attainable even though perfection is impossible. We are, perhaps, wiser than we were.

Through this half-century, developments in the more sheltered realm of moral philosophy have coincided with social and political trends in a way that may be disconcerting to those for whom philosophy is above and beyond the accidents of time and place and the common cares of ordinary experience. The nineteenth-century promise of a scientific ethics has met the fate of the nineteenth-century ideal of progress. All definitions of "good" were charged with committing the Naturalistic Fallacy. Moral philosophy was said to rest on a mistake. And finally all ethical theories and moral philosophy itself were declared dead—or bankrupt—when it was discovered that ethical judgments are "meaningless."

But the idea that moral behavior is rational, that reason is applicable to moral problems, has not remained buried. Even those who directed the funeral have assisted in the resurrection. But here, too, the revived theory cannot be identified with that which prevailed prior to the attacks by emotivism and irrationalism. This work is an attempt to state where we stand, now that the attack has slackened and its results can be assessed.

[1]

Ethical theories of every genre have been formulated and defended in our century, but perhaps the development most directly influential in determining the over-all pattern of twentieth-century moral philosophy, is one that, though its roots extend into the past, has its immediate beginning in G. E. Moore's *Principia Ethica*. Ethical intuitionism, Moore's positive theory in *Principia Ethica,* is of course merely a continuation of earlier theories and has exerted no decisive influence. It is rather those followers of Moore who could not accept intuitionism who have given moral philosophy its new look.

The crucial elements of Moore's book are the critical, not the constructive, ones. For one group of young philosophers Moore did not establish intuitionism, but he did destroy naturalism as a tenable position in ethical theory. The famous "open question" argument was accepted as a conclusive refutation of any attempt to define ethical predicates in terms of natural properties, and it was believed that such definitions were essential to ethical naturalism.

But, subsequently some of Moore's students found they could not "perceive" or "intuit" the simple, unanalyzable, nonnatural property that Moore claimed was denoted by "good." Or, and this was perhaps more decisive, some of them acquired empiricist prejudices that forbade their admitting the possible existence of any nonnatural property. Hence the "emotive theory" was born in Ogden and Richards' suggestion that in Moore's peculiar use of "good" "the word stands for nothing whatever, and has no symbolic function."

Once launched, the idea proved attractive to many and was frequently suggested as a means of solving some of the persistent problems of ethical theory. The restriction of the epithet "emotive" to Moore's particular use of "good" was, of course, soon abandoned, all the more readily because Moore's criticism was taken to have shown the fallacy of any other use. By the time of A. J. Ayer's *Language, Truth and Logic,* the suggestion was put forward as a sweepingly radical ethical theory, applicable to "every case in which one would commonly be said to be making an ethical judgment."

It is in Ayer's book that ethical theory as a legitimate field of philosophic inquiry is interred. For, Ayer declares, "ethical theory consists simply in saying that ethical concepts are pseudo-concepts and therefore unanalysable." All else is psychology, sociology, exhortation, or pure nonsense.

After the *succès de scandale* of Ayer's radical statement of the emotive theory, nothing remained for philosophers who were persuaded by the view but either to abandon ethics or begin qualifying the emotive theory. The subsequent history of this strand of twentieth-century moral philosophy is a history of successive qualifications that reinstate ethics as a proper domain of philosophical analysis and investigation.

The first major step in the restoration was C. L. Stevenson's *Ethics and Language,* which admitted that ethical terms might not be *completely* without cognitive content, but claimed their status as *ethical* terms depended upon a different kind of meaning, "emotive meaning," that Stevenson sought to analyze in detail.

But although Stevenson's work served to make the emotive theory more respectable, the very exhaustiveness of his analysis, and subsequent defenses of it, sufficed to exhibit the fruitlessness of this line of analysis. For the realization spread that a discussion of "meaning" was not the most useful way of approaching the problems of moral philosophy. Here, again, the influence of G. E. Moore can be seen; Moore had declared the fundamental task in ethical theory was to determine the meaning of (define) ethical terms. And this had been accepted without question by the emotive theorists. Once this bit of dogma was dislodged, work in a more fruitful vein began. Since the war, in articles and books by a number of writers including S. Toulmin, K. Baier, Henry Aiken, H. L. A. Hart, R. Hare, P. H. Nowell-Smith, among others, the real revolution (or at least the major development) in twentieth-century moral philosophy has occurred.

The crux of this revolution is the awareness that the fundamental error of philosophers in ethics is not that described by Moore's Naturalistic Fallacy, but is one committed by Moore and the emotive theorists as well as by the traditional theories Moore criticized. The error is to try to assimilate ethical discourse to a logical model that it will not fit, that is, the logic of scientific discourse. But where the traditional theories had mistakenly tried to make it fit, the emotivists had mistakenly thought all that could be said was that it did not fit.

The newly developing theory takes neither of these courses. The characteristic views distinguishing this theory from its predecessors are: (1) though the logic of moral discourse and the logic of scientific discourse are not identical, ethics need not therefore be illogical or irrational; (2) the proper object of analysis in moral philosophy is not the meaning of ethical terms, but the function or use of ethical statements or utterances; (3) this analysis can be fruitfully pursued only when the examination of these statements or utterances takes full account of their behavioral and linguistic contexts.

But once this basic orientation of the developing theory is made evident, it may perhaps be seen that the theory is not as revolutionary as it has seemed, or, and perhaps better, that this group of writers has not been alone in creating the new shape of moral philosophy in this century. For, perhaps less clearly perceived, or at least less clearly stated, a very similar basic orientation can be seen to underlie much of the writing of pragmatists in ethics. Thus two streams of philosophical thought which have been generally opposed may finally prove to be complementary rather than antagonistic.

But this was perhaps to be expected. One of the results of the development of the emotive theory was to drastically shift the locus of theoretical disagreement in a way that has been misleading. Traditionally, the most vigorously contested and most inconclusive disputes in moral philosophy have been between advocates of empirical and of nonempirical theories—between those who felt that, to be intelligible, morals must be grounded in human experience and permit of justification and correction by reference to that experience and those who held that, to be effective, morals must be understood as deducible from inviolable and incorrigible principles that are themselves given through metaphysical insight, revelation, or "intuition." Our century has seen a rather wholesale triumph of empiricism in philosophy and a consequent lessening of debate over metaphysical problems in ethics. This has not, however, led to any great decrease in either the number or vehemence of disagreements in moral philosophy; traditional disputes were soon replaced by a species of internecine warfare among empiricists, generated by the development of the emotive theory which in its radical form seemed to imply that a thorough adherence to empirical principles makes impossible any *reasonable* solution of moral problems. But one might have hoped that the basic commitment to empiricism uniting all of the parties to this dispute would eventually provide ground for a reconciliation. The current trend described above may indicate that this reconciliation is not as far distant as we had supposed.

It is my belief that empiricists need not disagree violently in moral philosophy, and that a united empiricism can provide a basis for an adequate ethical theory. The task I have undertaken in this study is to outline an ethical theory that combines, or has its roots in, both of what I take to be the two main streams of twentieth-century moral philosophy—pragmatism and the analytic movement I have attempted to describe above. Perhaps no one will agree that my version of this combination is correct, or even a combination at all. Be that as it may, I am convinced some such conjunction of these two streams will provide the next major development in moral philosophy.

I propose to begin my sketch of an ethical theory at what I take to be the proper starting point, though it is one from which starts are seldom made. This point is the question of *criteria* for an adequate ethical theory.

A rational choice between conflicting theories is possible only where there are some accepted criteria of adequacy for such theories. If we do not have a fairly definite notion of what sort of thing a theory is supposed to be and what it is supposed to do, we cannot of course tell whether a particular theory is a good one or better than some alternative. Hence, as a preliminary to agreement in moral philosophy, empiricists might be expected at least to agree on criteria for an adequate ethical theory. But even this has not been done, though failure here is perhaps owing less to actual disagreements over criteria than to the fact that few empiricists have attempted a formulation of such standards. Possibly most empiricists in ethics tacitly assume the same criteria, but until these are explicitly stated, one can neither judge them as criteria nor determine how well they are met by any theory. A first step toward an empiricist theory of ethics must be a statement of the criteria the theory is to satisfy.

But one cannot arbitrarily stipulate standards. Rather, the criteria themselves are open to question, and unless they are acceptable, the labor of constructing a theory to meet them may well be in vain. To what source, then, may one turn for such criteria as we seek? We might infer from previous theoretical constructions the criteria implicitly applied, or adopt without question those criteria we can find explicitly stated. Or we might instead try to derive criteria directly from the common fund of experience that is presupposed in any attempt at theorizing—experience of actual ethical problems and of moral discourse as it is used in the context of these problems. I shall adopt this last alternative.

Since all analyses of ethics presuppose a similar common sense experience of moral problems and language, we may have reason to hope that criteria proposed by common sense will at least have an initial plausibility. However, the criteria dictated by common sense may prove impossible to satisfy. They may, for example, be inconsistent, or they may be so vague or ambiguous as to defy any clear specification. Should this prove true, we must turn from common sense to ethical theory for a clarification; we must, as it were, filter common sense through the sieve of traditional ethical theory. And even should common sense criteria exhibit no such disqualifying characteristics, we may find it expedient to reduce a multiplicity of common sense criteria to a small number of essential requirements and to translate the language of

6

common sense into the perhaps more precise terminology of contemporary theory. But at all events, common sense must remain the primary source.

The search for criteria will, then, begin in sorting through some of the deliverances of common sense and the elements of common experience. In the light of much of current philosophical theory, this may seem quite like rummaging through old trunks long forgotten in the attic, but these trunks, like others, may harbor forgotten treasures. In chapter II I will seek to provide a background from which criteria may be drawn. In chapter III I shall attempt to formulate criteria that may be generally acceptable. The problem thereafter will be to find to what extent an empiricist theory can meet such criteria.

CHAPTER II

COMMON SENSE AND ETHICAL DISCOURSE

A NEUTRAL OBSERVER of the contemporary philosophical scene would be hard pressed to find among all the currently defended ethical theories one that does not somewhere claim to be in accord with common sense. Not only this, each also claims that common sense refutes all opposing theories. This implies that there is not one and only one clear "common sense notion" of ethics or morals any more than there is one and only one distinct meaning of terms in "ordinary usage." Precise concepts can be extracted from common sense or common usage only by shearing away or ignoring a great deal of the very common sense that is at the same time appealed to as authoritative. The justification frequently offered for this highly selective use of common sense as expressed in common usage is that the selected segment illuminates *a* or *the* "typical ethical sense" of a term.

But the history of moral theory makes it abundantly clear that recognition of a "typical ethical sense" is often confined to philosophers of a particular tradition or school, while philosophers of rival traditions find this sense not typical or, perhaps, not even ethical. Hence the searcher for generally acceptable criteria cannot base these upon "typical" senses drawn from one or two examples of moral discourse. He must instead seek quite general characteristics manifest in the whole broad range of common usage. What may be found in common usage is, perhaps, not meanings of particular terms or a set of common values, but rather the common *functions* of ethical language.

Long before any of us begin debating subtleties of ethical theory, we have heard, responded to, and used more or less correctly a large number of the terms philosophers call "ethical"—such terms as "good," "bad," "right," "wrong," "ought," "kind," "cruel," "honest," etc. We learn to use and to respond to uses of these terms in what should be a bewildering variety of circumstances, but we are in fact seldom bewildered at all. Such terms are incorporated into our linguistic habits without our finding it necessary first to have them defined or have their uses specified. We learn their uses by using them, and in learning to use them we learn also to engage in the peculiarly human activities of judging the worth of objects, the advisability of actions, the praise- or blame-worthiness of characters.

As we learn these linguistic patterns and perform these activities, we make no distinction between ethical and nonethical senses of the terms

8

or aspects of the activity. We speak of a great variety of objects and actions, and employ the same "ethical" terms for each. There are "good dogs," "good books," "good tools," "good halfbacks," "good men," "good causes," "good days," "good ideas," "good questions," "good judgments," "good deeds," and so on indefinitely; and of course, there are "better," "best," "bad," "worse," and "worst" of all these. There are "right roads," "right wrenches," "right decisions," "right answers," "right moves," "right companions," "right days," "right motives," "right feelings"; and for all these there are also "wrong" ones. We say "You ought not read without your glasses," "He ought to work harder," "You ought to have seen him," "I ought to go to bed," "You ought to keep your promise," "Lincoln ought to have lived longer," "They ought not to have spent their money so foolishly," "Everyone ought to read this book," "Hamlet ought to have acted sooner."

In many situations the choice of either "right," "ought," or some form of "good" is quite arbitrary; we can make substantially the same statement using any of the three. We may say, for example, "This is a good day for a picnic," "This is just the right day for a picnic," or "On a day like this, we ought to go on a picnic"; or we may say "Jones will make a good senator," "Jones is the right man for the senate," or "Jones is the man one ought to vote for for the senate"; or we may say "In the circumstances, the best thing to do is keep your promise," "The right act would be to keep your promise," or "You ought to keep your promise." Common usage in many instances makes no significant distinction between the three terms.

Generally, statements containing the term "right" are, in ordinary usage, replaceable by statements containing "good" or "the best" without change of meaning. We say "That was the right thing to do" or "That was the best thing to do," "He made the right decision" or "He made a good (the best) decision." The most common sort of exception to this generalization occurs when "right" picks out one particular act or object that meets some rather precisely specified requirements, as when we speak of "the right page" of a book or "the right address" or "the right amount of change."

We cannot, however, simply reverse the generalization and claim that any statement containing "good" is replaceable by a statement containing "right." The replacement can be made in many instances, of course, but in many it cannot. We cannot, for example, replace "He is a good doctor" with "He is the right doctor" or "That is a good refrigerator" with "That is the right refrigerator" except in contexts of decision making. Nor can we replace "That was the best car I ever owned" with any statement containing "right" without change of meaning. As a rule the uses of "good" for which there is no roughly equivalent use of "right" occur in statements expressing judgments of the general excellence or worth of a person or object in a context that does not involve choice or decision.

Most statements containing either "right" or "good" can also be replaced by statements containing "ought." This is true not only where uses of "good" and "right" are interchangeable, but applies generally to uses of "right" not replaceable by statements containing "good" and to many uses of "good" not interchangeable with uses of "right." For example, we may say either "That is the right address" or "That is the address you ought to have"; and in many contexts, even when no decision need be made, we make no distinction between "That is a good refrigerator" and "You ought to see that refrigerator," or "He is a good doctor" and "People ought to go to him" or "You ought to try him."

In accord with ordinary usage, then, the set of situations in which it is appropriate to utter a statement containing "good" and the set of situations in which it is appropriate to utter a statement containing "right" overlap, and, within the area of overlap, the "same thing" can be said using either term. Further, the use of "ought" is appropriate through almost the whole range of uses of "good" and "right." Where "good" does not overlap with uses of "right," it occurs in utterances expressing judgments of excellence or worth; where "right" does not overlap with uses of "good," it occurs in utterances stating that a specific requirement in the situation has been or may be met.

Where uses of "good" and "right" do overlap, the utterances may either be judgments of worth or statements about the fulfillment of requirements, *or both*. Thus either "That was a good meal" or "That was just the right meal" may, in the proper context, express the same judgment of excellence; "That is a good (the best) wrench for the job" or "That is the right wrench" state that requirements are met; while either "Jones is a good (the best) man for the Senate" or "Jones is the right man for the Senate" may both state that Jones satisfies certain requirements and express a judgment of worth. When *both* these functions are performed in a statement containing either "good" or "right," they may be related in one of two ways: either the excellence of the object enables it to meet the implied requirements, or the fact that it meets the requirements is the ground of its excellence. Usually the form of the relation cannot be determined without knowledge of the context of the utterance. Needless to say, in most conversational usage these two functions and their relations are not distinguished.

The term "ought" performs either function, or both: extending with uses of "right" to mere statements that requirements are met ("You ought to use the side door") and with "good" to mere judgments of worth ("You ought to taste that wine"), and covering the area of overlap where both functions are performed ("One ought to vote for Jones for Senator"). "Ought" is even more flexible in its usage than "right" or "good."

These characteristics of ordinary usage are independent of any distinction between ethical and nonethical senses of these terms. In the course of normal development, we do come to distinguish, if not moral from nonmoral uses of terms, at least moral from nonmoral problems. However, in our ordinary thoughts and habits, this distinction is but roughly drawn; lines of demarcation are not sharp and we do not often stop to classify our problems as moral or nonmoral. Ethical and non-ethical statements may sound alike and evoke much the same response in everyday life. Still, the distinction may emerge at any time if a statement is challenged or subjected to critical scrutiny; we can easily pick out problems and statements occurring in the context of such problems, which would be generally accepted as ethical or moral. What has been said about the uses of "good," "right," and "ought" in general can be seen to apply to their ethical usage as well.

Suppose, for example, that a man finds a billfold containing seven dollars and a driver's license identifying the owner, then hesitates between returning the billfold or spending the money to buy medicine for his sick wife. His would be a moral problem; the man becomes a moral agent. When he reaches a decision, he may express it equally well by "The best thing to do is to return the billfold," "The right thing to do is to return the billfold," or "The thing that ought to be done is to return the billfold." In this context the three forms have quite the same meaning. Thus it can be seen that clearly ethical usages occur in the area where "good," "right," and "ought" overlap. The question remaining is whether *all* ethical usages occur in this area.

Most of the ordinary ethical uses of "right" seem replaceable by uses of "good" or "ought." Statements asserting that some action is right, for example, "The right thing to do is . . . ," or "He did the right thing," generally, when taken in context, do not differ significantly from "That is a good (the best) thing to do" or from "That is what ought to be done." This is also true of applications of "right" to objects, persons, or characteristics. "They are not the right companions for him" has the same meaning as "They are not good companions for him" or "He ought not have these companions": and "The right attitude toward one's enemies is one of forgiveness" is much the same as "The best attitude toward one's enemies is one of forgiveness" and "One ought to have an attitude of forgiveness toward his enemies."

There seem, however, to be some ethical uses of "right" which merely assert that a requirement exists or will be satisfied by a particular action. In these "right" cannot be replaced by "good." Such uses frequently occur in discussions of hypothetical situations rather than in the context of actual problems. In a conversation on morals, for example, one may say "If a man makes a promise and he can keep it, then the *right* act is to keep it." Here exists a reference to the satisfaction of a requirement with no comparison of alternative actions. Still, ordinary usage does not always sharply distinguish this statement from "If ... then the best thing to do is to keep it." In the context of an actual problem, the two statements may be interchangeable.

Similarly, for most ethical uses of "good" there are equivalent uses of "right." Exceptions are such statements as "He is a man of good character," "Health is a greater good than money," mere judgments of worth usually made in contexts not involving actual choice or decision. These same statements may be invoked in contexts of decision, of course, but then they become interchangeable with "He has the right sort of character," "The right thing is to stay healthy, even without money," and so on.

This great flexibility of our ordinary usage of "good," "right," and "ought" is a primary source of the difficulty felt by those who would construct an ethical theory on the basis of definitions of one or more of these terms. If the terms are defined independently, we cannot easily explain the many uses in which they have the same meaning; yet if they are all defined in the same way, the contexts in which they are not interchangeable must be explained away, as in the emotive theory, which accounts for differences in usage by the rather unconvincing method of calling them mere "linguistic niceties" related to "slight emotive differences" in the terms.

But, it may be asked, if we are neither to begin nor end with definitions of these central ethical terms, what is to be the focus of ethical theory?

The preceding discussion of ordinary usage provides an answer. We have found that statements containing either "right," "good," or "ought," whether ethical or nonethical, serve one or both of two functions. They express judgments of worth or judgments about the existence or satisfaction of requirements. When these statements occur in the context of moral problems or discussions, we may call the first function that of expressing *evaluations* and the second that of ascribing *obligations*. Any of the three central ethical terms may appear in statements performing either function. At the focus of ethical theory, then, are these two functions of moral discourse and the underlying notions of *value* and *obligation*. In recent years this focus has been often somewhat blurred by those who would approach ethical theory through definitions of "right," "good," or "ought."

Our discussion has concentrated on the uses of these three terms, but in ordinary discourse the two functions are also performed by statements that contain none of these. Yet in the context of an ethical problem these are "ethical statements" in just the same way as are statements containing "good," "right," or "ought." This provides a further reason for attending directly to the functions performed rather than to particular terms that occur in the language of morals. Those who take the primary task of ethical theory to be that of defining particular terms tend to become involved in an endless and rather fruitless unraveling of different "senses" of these terms, almost to the point of losing the theory in a maze of subtle distinctions. And there still remains the task of relating ethical statements that contain none of these terms to the proper senses of the terms, that is, of somehow fitting such statements into the theory. But much of this can be avoided by attending directly to the characteristic functions of ethical statements; the feeling that different senses must be distinguished and the difficulty of making useful distinctions both stem from the fact that any of the ethical terms may be used for either function.

Ethical statements, regardless of the particular terminology in which they may be couched, characteristically perform one or both of two functions—expressing evaluations and ascribing obligations. Thus the primary concern of ethical theory is to explicate and analyze these two functions rather than to analyze particular ethical terms. In this section my aim is to explore the demands that common sense and common usage make upon the statements performing these functions.

In the context of a moral problem, language plays a variety of roles. Some utterances state the conditions of the problem; some formulate possible alternative actions; some give reasons for preferring one or another of these alternatives; some formulate rules or principles applicable in the situation; some state the decision finally reached, etc. Many of these utterances express evaluations or ascribe obligations. Common sense regards all these statements, in whatever role, as equally capable of being true or false. This is shown not only by the protest raised against theories that proclaim ethical statements to be neither true nor false, but also by our ordinary language habits. We indicate acceptance of a statement uttered in a moral context by saying "That's true," "That's so," "That's evident," "I know that": whereas, if we wish to reject or challenge the statement, we may say "That's not true," "That's hardly true," "What is your evidence for that?" "I doubt that," "Why should I believe that?"

Nothing in this common sense usage indicates ethical statements are regarded as being true or false in any different sense than are non-ethical statements. Our verbal responses are, in general, quite similar and our behavior follows the same pattern in either instance. If we accept a statement as true, we adjust our behavior to accord with it; if we doubt it, we seek justification and if satisfactory reasons are given, we then admit the assertion to be true. In this we make no apparent distinction between the way reasons are related to ethical statements and the way they are related to nonethical statements; in both instances we are ready to reject some reasons as irrelevant, to dismiss others as being of little weight, and to consider some fairly conclusive. And we usually acknowledge that there is some set of reasons sufficient to justify the statement in question.

Common sense provides little support for ethical theories that limit the meanings of ethical statements to assertions about the feelings, attitudes, or volitions of the speaker. It is a marked characteristic of our ordinary moral discourse that we may always ask for reasons for an ethical statement; and if no reasons can be given, we often cease to regard the statement as ethically significant. It is not that we reject it as false, though we sometimes do that. Rather, we expect ethical statements, like all factual statements, to be *grounded* and when someone utters what sounds like an ethical statement and fails to provide a ground, we cease to give the utterance serious consideration. Our usual treatment of ordinary empirical statements is very similar. If someone tells us that Soviet foreign policy is going to change, or that it will rain next week, we may ask, "What makes you think that?" "What evidence is there for that?" And if our informant can cite no evidence, but merely answers, as children do, "No reason, I just thought it up" or "I dreamed it last night" or "I just feel it," we refuse to take the assertion seriously. We do not reject it as false, since it may be true for all we know; we rather refuse to consider it as a genuine empirical statement.

Many ethical utterances not only function as evaluation or obligation statements but also give reasons ("Since John has displayed both honesty and courage, he ought to be rewarded"). But others only imply that there are reasons, which are left unspecified ("John ought to be rewarded"). It is *always* felt proper to ask for reasons for a statement of the latter sort, and if no reasons are forthcoming, we may refuse to take the statement as ethically significant, that is, we do not feel it necessary either to adjust our behavior to accord with it or to defend our failure to do so. But this is so not only when *no* reasons are given, but also when the reasons offered are statements about the feelings or attitudes of the speaker. It is this that indicates the common sense rejection of subjectivist ethical theories.[1]

This rejection in no way conflicts with our willingness to use, and accept, the dictates of conscience or "intuition" as reasons for an ethical judgment. Though "My conscience tells me" is a different sort of reason from those usually given in support of ordinary empirical statements, it *is* a reason. And when conscience or intuition is allowed to provide reasons for an ethical statement, these reasons are not thought to refer simply to the feelings or attitudes of the speaker; both conscience and intuition are regarded as sources, however mysterious, of objective knowledge and not as mere reflections of a psychological state. When we regard conscience and intuition merely as reflections of the psychological states of the speaker, we no longer are inclined to admit them as legitimate supports of ethical statements. Further, references to conscience or intuition are seldom the only reasons given, but most often occur in conjunction with factual statements describing the person, object, or action that is the subject of the ethical judgment.

Hence the frequently heard appeal to conscience or intuition in ordinary ethical discourse indicates neither a retreat to subjectivism nor the assertion of ethical statements for which reasons cannot be given.

Our habitual use of language in ethical situations reflects the common sense view that regards ethical statements as objective in the sense that they are not statements about the speaker's feelings or attitudes, they can be justified, and they cannot be justified merely by reference to the speaker's feelings and attitudes. Most often we are ready to reject as totally irrelevant any such assertion as "I approve of X" or "I like X" if offered as a reason for an ethical judgment; if such statements are admitted as relevant, they are usually given little weight and almost

---

[1] I use the term "subjective theory" in the sense specified by A. C. Ewing in *The Definition of Good* (New York: Macmillan, 1947), p. 2. In this sense, subjective theories include the following views: (1) that ethical judgments are not really judgments at all; (2) that they are all false or that we are never justified in thinking them true; (3) that they are merely judgments about the psychological state or dispositions of the speaker.

never accepted by themselves as sufficient reasons. On the other hand, assertions about the persons, objects, or actions that are the subjects of ethical statements are almost always accepted as relevant reasons. In common sense terms, ethical statements are statements about the objects referred to and not merely statements about the speaker or expressions of the speaker's attitudes. Utterances of the latter two types are not regarded as genuinely ethical.

One general common sense demand upon moral discourse, then, is that genuinely ethical statements must be grounded in knowledge of the object judged.

We further believe that acceptance of an ethical statement as true is, or should be, sufficient motivation for action. If we agree that anyone *ought* to perform some act, and he does perform it, we never consider it necessary to ask why he acted so. And if someone asserts that some act is good, right, or ought to be done, then we expect him either to act appropriately, explain his inability to do so, or apologize for failing to do so.

Ethical statements are felt as compelling and are used as instruments of compulsion, but the compulsion is usually intended to be impersonal, originating in the facts or requirements of the situation rather than in the will of the speaker. We do, of course, sometimes express purely personal demands in the language of ethics, saying "You ought to do this" when we have no reason other than "I want you to do this"; but once this is revealed, the use of "ought" is felt to be illegitimate and the authority claimed by the statement spurious.

We often do feel personal demands to be authoritative and respond to them as willingly and as promptly as to the impersonal demands of ethical statements. But the felt authority of a personal demand depends largely upon the prestige of the speaker and our relationship to him, whereas the authority of an ethical statement is generally independent of any particular speaker. A seeming exception to this is the speaker acknowledged to have moral authority whose statements, for that reason, carry more weight than do the words of ordinary men. But here, too, the ethical statement is not heard as a personal demand; rather, it is thought to issue from the superior moral knowledge or insight of the authoritative speaker.

In practice, ethical statements are frequently felt to be more compelling when the speaker is any person of prestige or authority. But we tend to attribute this again to the greater wisdom or experience of the speaker—if *he* says that something ought to be done, then it is most probably true that it ought to be done. But again, the demand remains impersonal and requires justification. We feel that unless the acts or attitudes urged upon us in ethical utterances can commend themselves to our reason, we are under no moral compulsion to comply, and we resent the use of ethical language to make unjustified or purely personal demands.

That we do resent what we feel to be an improper use supports the now familiar claim that ethical terms have an "emotive meaning." The terms "good," "right," "ought," etc., when uttered with the proper intonation, do tend to evoke feelings or attitudes of approval toward the objects so called. Our resentment is aroused when this power is abused, when these words are used to invoke our approval and then are not sustained and reinforced by being related to some actual requirement or merit. We do not feel resentful if the statement proves false, that is, if reasons are given which are shown to be false or otherwise insufficient. We may then consider the speaker mistaken, misguided, or a fool, but we do not consider his act an imposture, an enlisting of our approval under false pretences, as we do when no reasons are forthcoming. We then feel that a fraudulent claim has been made which somehow takes advantage of our moral nature.

This has been overlooked by emotive theorists. Amidst all the reputed vagueness and ambiguity of ethical terms, they have found one constant element, the expression of the speaker's approval, and have seized upon this as the meaning of ethical statements. But at least one other factor is equally constant; ethical statements are always understood to be supported by reason. They imply the claim made is one that a *reasonable* man would willingly allow. Ethical statements make claims upon us, but claims advanced as impersonal and rationally justifiable. We may grant the truth of the emotivists' insistence on the dynamic or magnetic character of ethical statements, and agree that they function to guide and influence attitudes and actions; but one of the characteristics which differentiate ethical statements from many other dynamic elements of language—exclamations and commands, for example—is the claim to be reasonable. "X is good" is never understood, in an ethical context, as "I approve of X, please do so as well," but rather as "X is deserving of approval, therefore approve." This is a condition of its being taken as an *ethical* judgment.

Common sense admits, indeed insists upon, a distinction between ethical statements and ordinary descriptive or scientific utterances. Most ethical statements have an immediate and direct connection with action; they are directly normative while ordinary descriptive statements affect our actions only indirectly.[2] The distinction made is one of function, but, as Dewey insisted, common sense does not construe this distinction as entailing a difference in structure and content. Rather it treats statements of both types as equally in need of and capable of justification, and considers action in accord with either to be reasonable only when the statement is in some degree justified.

In this chapter I have tried to explore some primary aspects of the language of ethics, to discern what ethical statements are ordinarily taken to communicate and what demands common sense makes upon any statement purported to be ethical. I have hoped that a clear answer to these questions might be instrumental in the formulation of criteria for an adequate ethical theory. I shall here review the common sense doctrine, leaving discussion of the suggested criteria to the next chapter.

Ethical statements in ordinary discourse function primarily to direct attitudes and actions. The common sense view does not take this function to be performed directly by the sounds themselves independent of any meaning they may have, nor by the infectious expression of the speakers' attitudes, but rather to be mediated by the communication of a content. It is thought to be the acceptance of the communicated content that produces a change in action or attitude.

The content of the communication is always one or both of two sorts of "fact"; either an action, object, state of affairs, or character is asserted to have a degree of value or disvalue, or some agent is asserted to be subject to certain requirements that may be satisfied by particular actions. In our earlier terminology: ethical statements are *evaluation statements* or *obligation statements*. In some instances common sense clearly distinguishes these two types of statement; more often it does not. In many circumstances ethical statements communicate "facts" of both types.

Both evaluation statements and obligation statements, if they are to be treated as genuinely ethical, must be grounded in knowledge of the situation judged, that is, in empirical statements describing the particular situation. Common sense places no restriction on the range of statements that may be taken as relevant, in general, although in each particular situation criteria of relevance may be invoked. Except in special circumstances, statements about the feelings and attitudes of the speaker are considered irrelevant or of little weight.

[2] For a more detailed discussion of this distinction between directly and indirectly normative statements, see A. Sesonske, " 'Cognitive' and 'Normative,' " *Philosophy and Phenomenological Research*, XVII (1956), 9.

Both evaluation statements and obligation statements are commonly regarded as providing motivation for action. They are recognized as dynamic, compelling, authoritative. But no statement is admitted as genuinely ethical unless its felt authority is justifiable, unless the demand made is shown or believed to be a reasonable demand and not merely an expression of personal whim or caprice.

These I take to be fundamental common sense beliefs about the language of ethics as they are expressed in our ordinary linguistic habits and behavior. These beliefs, and these facts of linguistic behavior, form a starting point for any analysis of moral discourse and any formulation of an empiricist ethical theory. Any radical departure from them must point out where common sense has erred and explain the persistence of the error.

CHAPTER III

CRITERIA FOR AN ADEQUATE
ETHICAL THEORY

THE PRECEDING DISCUSSION was intended to serve as a background from which we might draw a minimum set of criteria for an adequate ethical theory. These criteria are designed as only necessary and not sufficient conditions for the correctness of an ethical theory. A theory that meets them may yet be incorrect or incomplete in other respects.

There are, of course, some criteria that must be met by theories of any sort and that are thus not specifically criteria for an ethical theory any more than they are criteria for, say, an adequate theory of perception. These include the criterion of logical consistency and the requirements entailed in our commitment to empiricism, that is, that there be no admission of nonnatural properties or synthetic a priori propositions. These general criteria are not here in question; it is, rather, the specific criteria for an ethical theory which are in doubt.

Twentieth-century philosophers have often asserted or assumed the primary requirement for an ethical theory to be to provide analyses or definitions of the "ethical terms," usually "good" and "right." This has been the view, for instance, of G. E. Moore, Sir David Ross, A. C. Ewing, A. J. Ayer, and C. D. Broad; and C. L. Stevenson states of his *Ethics and Language* (p. 1), "Its first object is to clarify the meaning of the ethical terms. . . ." But our ordinary usage of these terms precludes either a clear distinction between "good" and "right" or an identification of them; hence a concentration on the particular terms has tended to lead into the blind alley of endlessly-multiplying subtle distinctions of differing "senses." What does emerge from common usage is not a set of distinctively ethical terms to be analyzed, but two characteristic communicative functions, two types of content that ethical statements are commonly believed to convey, which are not dependent on any particular terminology.

Accordingly, we may take the primary common sense demand upon any ethical theory to be that it provide a systematic interpretation of these two functions, that it analyze the two fundamental types of ethical statements. An adequate ethical theory must, then, contain analyses both of judgments of evaluation and of judgments of obligation.

Common sense not only sets this as the task of ethical theory, but also provides criteria for these analyses in the conditions it requires a judgment to meet if the judgment is to be ethically significant. The characteristics commonly deemed necessary in an ethical judgment are: (1) that it be grounded in knowledge of the situation; (2) that it have a felt motivational force; that is, that it be taken as *authoritatively* directing specific attitudes or actions; (3) that the judgment be justifiable, or capable of being warranted. Thus the criteria for an ethical theory implied in our common responses to ethical situations are: (1) the theory must provide analyses of both judgments of evaluation and judgments of obligation; and in each instance it must (2) provide a *grounding* for the judgment; that is, it must show the relationship between the ethical judgment and the empirical or scientific statements that "support" it; (3) it must account for the *felt motivational force* of the judgment; that is, it must elucidate the characteristics of these judgments by virtue of which they do, as a matter of fact, have this felt, immediate force; (4) it must provide a *warrant* for the judgment; that is, it must provide a method of justification.

These criteria are implied in our ordinary use of language and in the demands commonly made in the actual context of moral discourse. But they are also the criteria that ethical theories have traditionally sought to meet. Every ethical theory has recognized and attempted to meet *some* of these criteria, but I am aware of none that has stated them all explicitly and kept them distinct. In order to show clearly that this is so, I shall briefly discuss each criterion with reference to the way it has been treated in the past.

A—.*An adequate ethical theory must provide analyses both of judgments of evaluation and judgments of obligation.* By a judgment of *evaluation* I mean a judgment of worth or excellence, an appraisal. In our everyday life we constantly make such judgments. We judge this book worth reading, this picture worth seeing, this item offered for sale not worth the price asked, this horse better than that, this man to be a scoundrel, and that one most worthy of admiration. Some of these judgments explicitly involve a comparison whereas others seem to assert the absolute worth of something in terms of its conformity to certain standards of excellence.

Obviously, not all judgments of worth are commonly considered to be ethical judgments, but many ethical judgments are of this type. An appraisal of a man's character is usually an ethical judgment, as are comparisons of alternative possible actions or goals of action in some situations, for example, when one attempts to decide to which of several charities to contribute.

By a judgment of *obligation* I mean a judgment asserting that some agent (or group or class of agents) has a duty or an obligation to perform some act (or type of act), that it is a requirement he is *bound* to fulfill. Judgments of obligation are also common in daily life, though perhaps not as frequent as are judgments of evaluation. We assert that we have an obligation to help defend our country, it is a duty to obey the law, when one agrees to undertake a task he has an obligation to complete it, and so on. Most judgments of obligation are, at least in a broad sense, ethical judgments, though a distinction is often made between legal and moral obligation.

All ethical judgments are either judgments of obligation or judgments of evaluation, or in some way combine the two functions. But in our ordinary language habits we make no clear distinction between the two. Rather we use the same so-called "ethical terms" to express judgments of either type. We say "You ought to keep your promise" or "It would be right to keep your promise," meaning in either instance "You *have an obligation to* keep your promise." We also say "You ought to have companions more your own age" or "The right companions would be some more your own age," and both statements mean "It *would be better if* you had companions more your own age." And in many instances the same utterance conveys judgments of both evaluation and obligation. This duality of common usage leads to confusion both in our ordinary discussions of ethical problems and in our excursions into ethical theory.

In ordinary discussions it leads us often to mistake judgments of one type for those of the other, and to argue for or against them on this basis. Thus often ensues a particularly frustrating sort of disagreement in which each party finds the other extremely obtuse and cannot understand why his own obviously true contentions are not convincing. A headstrong youth might, for example, take the assertion "You ought to have companions more your own age" as a judgment of obligation and reject it, and any arguments for it, on the ground that he was perfectly free to choose any companions he pleased. He might even grant that companions his own age would be better for him, but still reject the original statement on the ground that he has no obligation to choose *good* companions, but is free even to choose *bad* companions if he wishes. But the judgment, *as a judgment of evaluation,* in no sense denies this freedom of choice. Rather, it asserts that if this freedom be exercised wisely, then choice of a certain type will result. But this judgment of evaluation is identical in appearance with the judgment of obligation that was rejected, and we are not always careful enough to make the correct interpretation, even of our own judgments.

In ethical theory this ambiguity of common usage has likewise made easy a confusion of the two types of judgment with resulting confusion in analysis. Philosophers have often taken ethical judgments to be all of one type, and hence have thought that one analysis would suffice for ethical theory. There have been philosophers who treat all ethical judgments as judgments of evaluation and limit the task of ethical theory to analysis of these, for example, Aristotle; those who tend to treat all ethical judgments as judgments of obligation and construct a theory almost wholly concerned with these, for instance, Kant; and philosophies that simply reduce both to a common denominator as, for example, the theory proposed by Ayer in *Language, Truth and Logic,* which makes no distinction at all between the types of judgment, but simply asserts all ethical judgments to be mere expressions of emotion.

Often the two aspects of evaluation and obligation have been recognized but have been fused together; ethical statements were thought to refer to values one has a duty to pursue or to acts possessing value because they are duties. All ethical uses of "good" have been taken as implying an obligation and all ethical uses of "right" as making an evaluation. It is this hybrid sense of these terms which has, I think, been asserted to be "indefinable," and has thus proven so troublesome for naturalists or empiricists in ethics.

It is my belief that drawing a clear and continually heeded distinction between judgments of evaluation and judgments of obligation will help clarify many of the puzzling problems of ethical theory. This distinction is not only necessary if we are to consider and analyze particular judgments of each type, but is also crucial in any analysis of those judgments that combine the two functions; for the relationship, within a single judgment, between evaluation and obligation can only be ascertained if we can first clearly single out the two aspects to be related. Therefore, since we commonly use the same terms in formulating either sort of judgment, I shall use a notation which will allow a continued use of common terminology and yet will plainly mark the distinction. When the terms "good," "right," and "ought" occur in judgments of *evaluation,* I shall write them "good$_e$," "right$_e$," and "ought$_e$"; when they occur in judgments of *obligation,* I shall write them "good$_o$," "right$_o$," and "ought$_o$." When consideration of statements that combine the functions is necessary, I shall introduce a suitable notation.

It is fairly obvious that both traditional and contemporary ethical theories have recognized at least one aspect of this first criterion, and have taken the primary task of ethical theory to be analysis of obligation, or of evaluation, or both. An awareness of the necessity for both analyses is perhaps more evident in the critical writings of philosophers than in the ethical theories offered. Each time a theorist has seemed to confine his attention purely to one type of judgment, or to reduce one to the other, critics have assailed the theory by pointing out that it fails to give an adequate account of a major portion of moral discourse and the moral life. Thus critics of Kant have proclaimed that his theory gives no account of, or leaves no place for, the Good and the common goods of life, and critics of Utilitarianism dwell on the weakness of this theory's treatment of obligation. Of course, those theories which explicitly attempt to reduce one sort of judgment to the other are, in so doing, offering analyses of both judgments of evaluation and of obligation, and so meet the criterion. But even so they have often been criticized for not adequately treating one aspect of moral discourse.

Writers like Ross and the British deontologists who have insisted that neither "right" nor "good" was reducible to the other, plainly recognize that an ethical theory must analyze two types of judgment and have found this requirement implied in our common opinions of moral matters. But writers of this persuasion have been misled by the duality of common usage into finding it necessary to appeal to nonnatural properties as denotata of ethical terms; hence their theories have been rejected by empiricists—the insights along with the errors.

Contemporary empiricists have tended to concentrate on judgments of evaluation. This is indicated by the current tendency to use "ethical judgment" and "value judgment" almost interchangeably, or at least to call all ethical judgments "value judgments." C. I. Lewis, among contemporary empiricists, has most clearly seen that an ethical theory must analyze two sorts of judgments, and that these call for quite distinct analyses. He has published a carefully worked-out and perceptive analysis of judgments of evaluation, but then insisted these are not yet ethical judgments, though an analysis of value and evaluation is a necessary prolegomenon to any ethical theory. Ethical theory proper, presumably, will deal with judgments of obligation.

B—.*In each instance the analysis must provide a ground for the judgment.* Every singular ethical judgment, that is, judgment of the type "It was wrong of John to take that money" as contrasted with judgments of the type "Stealing is wrong," is subject to the demand that reasons be given. Often the "reasons" actually given will include universal ethical statements such as "Stealing is wrong," but they must also always include empirical statements about the person or situation judged. Following Stevenson's usage in *Ethics and Language,*

I shall limit the term "reason" to these empirical statements offered in support of an ethical judgment.

One of the demands made by common sense upon the language of morals is that all ethical judgments must be grounded in such reasons, these reasons being ordinarily understood as related in some way to the truth or falsity of the judgment. For example, if it should be asserted "It was wrong of John to take the money," we should ordinarily think the empirical statement "The money belongs to Jim" to be somehow relevant to the truth of the judgment; but if it were shown that the money really belongs to John, this would be taken as tending to prove the judgment false.

This criterion demands that an adequate ethical theory give some account of the grounding of ethical judgments; that is, it should analyze the relations that may hold between an ethical judgment and the reasons that support or refute it.

Much work by contemporary thinkers has been directed toward making clear the nature of these relations. John Dewey has argued that value statements can and must be grounded in empirical statements, contending that these empirical statements assert causal connections which form the basis for the evaluation of an action in relation to an end to be reached. We assert an action to be "good" when our experience and tested observations lead us to believe causal relations are such that the proposed action will probably lead to an intended end.[1] Hans Reichenbach has also noted that in many instances the relationship is of the sort with which Dewey has been so concerned; empirical statements establish causal relationships that are then logically related to an ethical judgment which itself is a statement about the relation of means to ends. But he has further insisted not all ethical judgments are of this hypothetical type.[2]

Perhaps the most meticulous treatment of the problem of the relation of reasons to ethical judgments is Stevenson's with its detailed consideration of many examples and many types of disagreement. Stevenson's theory is perhaps unique in the history of ethical theory in that he offers his reader a choice in the type of relation that holds here. In his first pattern of analysis, in all but a few unusual instances, the relationship between judgment and reason is held to be merely psychological. But in the second pattern it is logical; and we are, Stevenson holds, generally free to interpret any ethical judgment in accord with either pattern.[3]

---

[1] *Theory of Valuation* (Chicago: University of Chicago Press, 1939), p. 23.

[2] *The Rise of Scientific Philosophy* (Berkeley and Los Angeles: University of California Press, 1951), pp. 297 ff.

[3] *Ethics and Language* (New Haven: Yale University Press, 1945), pp. 227–231.

C—.In each instance the analysis must account for the felt, immediate force of the judgment. At least part of what philosophers have meant by calling some statements "normative" is that the statements as ordinarily used are compelling, authoritative, dynamic; they are felt as prods to action. Thus this criterion may be restated as: In each instance the analysis must account for the felt normative force of the judgment. This criterion is concerned with the psychological rather than the logical conditions of ethical judgments; it can be satisfied only by some explication of the relationship between such judgments and the feelings, emotions, and attitudes commonly connected with them.

The authors of the emotive theory of ethics have marked out this criterion as central and have sought to meet it with their analysis of the "emotive meaning" of ethical terms. Although this characteristic of some words to be "emotive" was noted by Berkeley and others, it has only recently been considered of any importance in ethical theory.

We have again to turn to Stevenson's writings for the most explicit and detailed recent attempt to meet this third criterion. His analysis of emotive meaning has roused some to question whether it can legitimately be called a form of *meaning* at all, but few have denied that some words do have the tendencies or dispositions Stevenson attributes to them.

Pragmatists have sought to meet this criterion in a different way by relating the felt authority or necessity of the judgment to the demands of the practical situation in which the judgment is made and to the felt necessity of the existential and known causal connections on which the judgment is based.[4] The value statement is taken to be concerned with a means–ends relation; it is, in Kant's terms, a hypothetical imperative. As such, the felt compulsiveness of the judgment derives from the felt need or desire for the end in question.

D—.In each instance the analysis must provide a warrant for the judgment. This criterion only iterates the demand commonly made of all statements put forth as assertions, ethical judgments along with others. If a statement of any sort, dealing with any subject matter, claims our assent and a place in our structuring of the world, if it pretends to be a conveyor of knowledge or wisdom (in any sense of these terms) and a reliable guide in action, then it is always subject to the demand that it be justified, that it be shown to be a *warranted assertion.* We do not actually make this demand of every assertion. Rather we usually rely on our knowledge of the veracity and reliability

---

[4] Cf. Sidney Hook, "The Desirable and Emotive in Dewey's Ethical Theory," in *John Dewey: Philosopher of Science and Freedom* (New York: Dial, 1950), p. 203; cf. *also* John Dewey, *Theory of Valuation,* chap. iv.

of the speaker as a guarantee of a warrant for the statement, particularly when the speaker is known to be competent and we are aware of no reason why he should deceive us. But the possibility of a demand for justification remains in every instance, and is actualized whenever a doubt arises.

All ethical theories have either implicitly or explicitly recognized this criterion, and have sought to meet it in one way or another. In the context of a fully specified set of criteria, we may be able to see more clearly than has previously been seen what is involved in the demand that a warrant be provided for ethical judgments. It is not only the cognitive content of the judgment which must be warranted, but also its authority, its "normative force." Criterion (3) required an explanation of the felt force of ethical judgments, but if the judgment is to be fully warranted, it is not enough merely to explain how it happens that we *feel* compelled to heed the judgment; it must also be shown that it is *reasonable* to heed it and to accept it as compelling.

In the past it has generally been assumed that the sort of justification that could be provided for ethical judgments was not radically different from that provided for any judgment. That is, it was thought an ethical judgment could be warranted or justified by being shown to be true— in the same sense as statements about the physical world are true. But many contemporary writers assert that ethical judgments are not capable of being true or false, in any empirical sense, and that if they were shown to be true or false, this would not suffice to justify them as *normative statements*. Hence the problem of justification has become central in contemporary moral philosophy and is perhaps the main point of contention among empiricists concerned with ethical theory.

The noncognitive theories, both emotive and conative, maintain that this criterion cannot be met if one is to remain an empiricist and if the criterion is understood to demand a *logical* justification of ethical judgments. But they have not abandoned the criterion entirely; they have instead argued that a *psychological* justification is all that can be given and need be given, and have attempted to present such a psychological justification. As a further development, some writers now hold that, although ethical judgments are not empirically true or false nor logically related to reasons in the same way evidential statements are related to probable conclusions, there is nevertheless a well-ordered and recognized method of justification of ethical judgments, a method no less logical merely for differing from the method of justification of scientific statements.[5]

---

[5] For example, S. Toulmin, *Reason in Ethics* (Cambridge: Cambridge University Press, 1950).

We may also remark that the justification of ethical statements may not be the same in all instances; we must distinguish between judgments and principles and perhaps use different methods of justification for each. Recent investigations of the notion of justification in general have held: If the ultimate principles of ethics can be only "pragmatically" justified, this is not peculiar only to ethics but is true of the ultimate principles of knowledge as well. This common distinction between judgments and principles has sometimes been overlooked and a single method of justification demanded to suffice for both. When this was not forthcoming, ethics was declared to be noncognitive. If empiricists are to formulate an adequate ethical theory, they must refrain from making impossible demands and then declaring the whole enterprise bankrupt when these cannot be met.

If it is evident that contemporary philosophers have implicitly adopted the criteria for an adequate ethical theory set forth here, it is equally evident they have done so without attempting any clear formulation of criteria, and they have, as often as not, confused the criteria in ways that have had unfortunate effects on the ensuing theory.

Perhaps the most common concomitant of a failure to specify clearly what criteria a theory is required to meet is the tendency to combine, unknowingly, two requirements in a single implicit criterion, which then cannot satisfactorily be met because each of the unrecognized components requires a different treatment. Two confusions of this sort have been particularly disruptive of the efforts made in recent empirical ethical writings: one a confusion of the requirement (2) that a *ground* be provided for the ethical judgment, namely, that the theory analyze the relation that holds between the judgment and its supporting reasons, with the requirement (4) that a *warrant* be provided, a method of justification be specified; the other a confusion of the requirement that (1) the theory provide an analysis of *judgments of obligation* with the requirement that (3) the analysis account for the *felt immediate force* of the judgment.

The criteria (2) and (4) both have to do with the way ethical judgments are related to our knowledge and experience; hence it may be natural that the difference between them has not always been discerned. The confusion has emerged in converse forms. On one side, it has been thought that no provision of a ground for the judgment could be satisfactory unless the *same* provision also sufficed to justify the judgment; on the other, it has been thought that no justification for an ethical judgment was necessary beyond the provision of a ground.

The noncognitive theorists have made the first form of this confusion central in their theory. The major point in their argument against cognitive theories has been the claim of lack of logical connection between an ethical judgment and the reasons given in support of it. This is asserted to be shown by the fact that no amount of empirical reasons entails the ethical judgment, or in the old, now familiar, terms, two persons may agree on all the facts of a situation, make no errors of logic, and yet arrive at different ethical conclusions. We may now see this as a contention that empirical reasons are not *sufficient* as a *warrant* for ethical judgments. We also see it as an indication that noncognitivists have taken the assertion that ethical judgments must be *grounded* in empirical statements to mean ethical judgments must be *justified* solely by reference to empirical statements. And when, rightly or wrongly, they found this could not be done, they asserted such judgments could not be rationally justified at all, thus demonstrating that they made no distinction between the two criteria (2) and (4).

The converse error is that indulged in by those empirical theorists who commit what G. E. Moore has misleadingly named the Naturalistic Fallacy. These philosophers take ethical terms to be synonymous with some set of terms denoting specific empirical properties. The empirical reasons for the ethical judgment are then taken to support the judgment by asserting or presenting evidence that the thing judged has these properties. Thus the theories provide a ground for the judgment; they show how it may be based on empirical statements. But they then assume that the judgment has also, by this fact, been warranted, that no further justification is called for or needed. And it is here the critics demur. They will admit, as does Ayer, that "good" may be used in a "descriptive sense," and then evidence making it probable that, say, an action will lead to the greatest pleasure of the greatest number, also tends to prove the action "good," in this sense. But, the critics contend, it does not prove that one "ought" to perform the action: it does not justify the directive character of the ethical judgment.

We have seen that in order for an ethical judgment to be fully warranted or justified, it must be shown that it is reasonable to accept the judgment as compelling. It is this which these "naturalistic" theories purportedly fail to do. It may be added that the intuitionistic theories which so loudly decry the naturalistic fallacy fail, themselves, in the same way. The substitution of a nonnatural property for the natural ones "good" is said to denote demonstrates in no way that I "ought to desire" the objects said to have this property.

Like the noncognitivists, these theorists have not plainly discerned that *two* criteria are to be met, (2) and (4), and, although logically (2) must be met before (4) can be satisfied, it is not necessary for a theory to attempt to satisfy (2) in a fashion which, in itself, also suffices for (4). It is not only not necessary, but I believe it is not possible if the theory is to be applicable to all ethical statements.[6] The recurrent criticism levelled at all these theories at least indicates that an adequate ethical theory that does not distinguish the two criteria has not yet been formulated.

The second prevalent tendency toward a confusion of criteria—a confounding of the requirement of criteria (1), an analysis of judgments of obligation must be given, with criteria (3), the theory must account for the felt immediate force, the expressive–incitive character, of the judgment—has its roots in the ambiguity of the language of ethical theory. Philosophers of whatever stripe, who have taken an interest in ethical theory, all concur in asserting that ethical statements, or at least "distinctively" ethical statements, are *normative*. This is true of both judgments of evaluation and judgments of obligation. And though there is no one precise generally-accepted meaning of "normative," a constant component of its varying senses is normative statements have a felt authority, or, as is often said, they tell us what we *ought* to do. The nature of this "ought" generally remains unspecified, but it nevertheless forms the psychological basis for the oft-expressed view that a characteristic of all ethical statements is they are "obligatory" or "binding." It has then been assumed that an analysis of this "obligatory" character of all ethical judgments suffices as an analysis of judgments of obligation, or, in other words, there is here only one criterion to be satisfied.

Morton White's critical article, "Value and Obligation in Dewey and Lewis," appears as an instructive example of this type of confusion. White considers here Dewey's attempt in *The Quest for Certainty* to distinguish the *desired* from the desirable in naturalistic terms, and he finds the attempt fails. White's conclusion is "Dewey . . . has not given us a naturalistic account of obligation." He further adds, "We may safely say, therefore, that pragmatism is still without a solution of the fundamental problem of ethics," namely, the problem of obligation.[7]

These conclusions indicate that White takes Dewey to be concerned with the problem of obligation, to be, in our terms, offering an analysis of judgments of obligation. This is indeed *a*, if not *the*, fundamental

[6] Cf. chap. iv, pp. 39 ff., and chap. v, pp. 88 ff.

[7] In Wilfrid Sellars and John Hospers, eds., *Readings in Ethical Theory* (New York: Appleton-Century-Crofts, 1952), p. 333.

problem of ethics. But it is not the problem Dewey is attacking in the particular chapter White criticizes. In this chapter, which is, significantly, entitled "The Construction of Good," Dewey is wholly concerned with judgments of evaluation. What White takes for an analysis of obligation is instead an explication of the normative character of judgments of evaluation; it is an attempt by Dewey in analyzing judgments of evaluation to meet criterion (3) and one of the requirements of (4). That is, Dewey is trying to account for the felt normative force of judgments of evaluation and to show the conditions under which it is reasonable to accept a judgment of evaluation as compelling.

Dewey never explicitly states this to be the intention of his discussion, and some of his remarks may, indeed, be interpreted as indicating that he did, as White believes, intend to undertake an analysis of obligation. But once we have set forth the criteria for an adequate ethical theory and clearly distinguished the several requirements made, it becomes apparent, I believe, that, whatever his intentions, what Dewey has actually done is offer an analysis of *judgments of evaluation* that attempts to meet all of these criteria.

Dewey's declared concern is to point out "the difference between the enjoyed and the enjoyable, the desired and the desirable, the satis*fying* and the satis*factory*."[8] The sort of judgment for which he offers an analysis is then taken by White, correctly, to be exemplified by "*a* is desirable." As Dewey makes clear, an adequate analysis must explicate the sense of "desirable" which has a "*de jure* quality." In this sense "desirable" designates not what *is* desired but what is *worthy of being desired*. But clearly the judgment "*a* is worthy of being desired" is a judgment of evaluation, and the *de jure* quality in question is the felt authority of the statement, the "normative" character of a judgment of evaluation. The notion of *obligation* is not involved here at all.

What leads White to believe Dewey is offering an analysis of judgments of obligation is that White translates "*a* is desirable" into "*a* ought to be desired." This is indeed an admissible translation, but since, as we have seen, "ought" occurs both in judgments of evaluation and in judgments of obligation, the translation remains ambiguous until the "ought" is identified as either "ought$_e$" or "ought$_o$." If we take "ought to be desired" to be synonymous with "worthy of being desired," as Dewey takes it, then it is plainly an "ought$_e$." White, without distinguishing the two senses, takes it to be an "ought$_o$." But we need only make this explicit in the judgment to see that it cannot be the sense intended by those who use the phrase. For, when translated it becomes:

8 "The Construction of Good," in Sellars and Hospers, *op. cit.*, p. 275.

"a is desirable" means "a is an obligatory object of desire," or when the judgment is addressed to a person, "You have an obligation to desire a."

In our ordinary discourse desires and feelings are not the sort of things said to be obligatory. We have obligations to *act* in certain ways, but not to have certain feelings. We may be said to have an obligation to keep a promise, pay a debt, speak the truth, aid a friend, but we do not often talk of having obligations to desire certain objects or to have certain feelings. Sometimes we do, as White does, say of some objects that they "ought to be desired," or when someone claims he does not desire what we think to be desirable, we may tell him, "You ought to desire it." But when we attempt to explain these statements in other terms we say the object is "a fitting object of desire" or "worthy of desire," or tell a person he would desire the object or state of affairs if he were wise, or knew what was best for him. But we do not say he has an obligation to desire it.

What gives plausibility to the notion that we may be obligated to have certain feelings or desires is the fact that we often do have obligations to *perform such actions* as will lead to our having these desires in the future, actions which will be instrumental to the formation of a character possessing the proper (?) desires. But that we ought$_o$ perform these actions does not alter the fact that we only ought$_e$ have these desires. The ground of our assertion that we ought$_o$ perform the actions lies in these facts, that we ought$_e$ have these desires and that in some circumstances we have an obligation to perform some acts productive of good.[9]

White has not thought to distinguish "ought$_o$" from "ought$_e$" and so has not seen the difference between an analysis of "ought$_o$" and an attempt to account for and justify the felt authoritative character of "ought$_e$." He is quite correct, then, in asserting that Dewey has not here given a satisfactory analysis of obligation. But this is hardly to be wondered at, since it is doubtful whether this is what Dewey meant to be doing.[10] White does not, in this paper, consider that Dewey may have given his account of obligation elsewhere.

For White, Dewey's chapter constitutes another naturalistic attempt to deal with the fundamental problem of ethics, the problem of obliga-

---

[9] For a discussion of these circumstances, and a further defense of the position taken here, see chap. v.

[10] If Dewey did intend his account of "desirable" to be an analysis of obligation, then he has, of course, fallen into the same confusion as has White. But even so, if we consider what Dewey's chapter *does*, rather than what it is intended to do, it may be seen as a plausible explication of "ought$_e$" rather than an implausible account of "ought$_o$."

tion. When taken as such the chapter lays itself, and naturalism, open to the recurring charge that naturalism has not yet offered a satisfactory analysis of obligation and that naturalistic theories never seek to explain the facts of obligation, but only to explain them away. As long as naturalists continue to confuse the two criteria (1) and (3), there will be some justice in the charge. For the problem of obligation, in the sense in which it is *a,* or *the,* fundamental problem of ethics, is not the problem of explaining how some statements happen to be felt as authoritative or what linguistic devices we may employ to persuade those who do not happen to feel this authority. Rather, it is the problem of stating under what conditions it may be correctly asserted that someone *has an obligation* to perform some act.

The cause of empiricism in ethics has suffered much from the failure of its adherents to enunciate criteria for their ethical theories and the consequent confusion of the various components of an adequate analysis. It has been nonempiricists, on the whole, who have been most responsive to the demands of common sense that confront any endeavor to systematize ethical discourse. But then nonempiricists have become so entangled in the ambiguities of common usage that they have been led to offer theories which really do not provide solutions for any of the perplexing problems, but merely put them aside. Empiricists have righteously, though rightly, rejected these theories along with the metaphysics which accompany them, but they have erred in also rejecting the common sense ethical attitudes which motivated these theories.

In these two chapters I have tried to determine some of the most persistent and uncompromising of these common sense ethical attitudes and to reinstate them as criteria for an adequate ethical theory. It is my conviction, if once these criteria are acknowledged and distinguished, one from the other, it may be seen that an ethical theory can be formulated which will be acceptable both to empiricists and to common sense. Such a theory will probably not satisfy those who demand that ethical statements be certain, or who feel life is futile and meaningless unless there is a guaranteed hierarchy of eternal values. For the best an empiricist theory can offer are probable statements and values grounded in the contingent facts of human needs and aspirations. What then remains is the task of trying to convince doubters such a theory is the only sort warranted by experience, and no other is needed.

In the remaining chapters of this study I shall try to develop an empiricist ethical theory that meets the criteria enunciated. In doing so I shall seek to avoid what seems to me the major failure of contemporary ethical theories—a tendency toward oversimplification. Empiricists have been inclined to treat ethical statements as if they were all of a piece, as if one analysis of a "typical ethical statement" would suffice for the whole range of ethical discourse. This inclination may have been inherited from traditional views which postulated a single authoritative source for all values and all duties, but it is surely not becoming in a philosophy dedicated to respect for the facts of experience. For any serious examination of the empirical facts of language usage will surely disclose that moral discourse, like the rest of the world, is made up of a number of things; there are a variety of ethical forms not reducible to one. A theory admitting of this variety of forms may not be as elegant as some would prefer, but it will be better able to meet the criticisms habitually levelled at empiricist theories.

The theory I shall propose will be neither "cognitive," "emotive," nor "volitional," as these terms have been currently used, since cognitions, emotions, and volitions will all be seen to have an essential role in ethical discourse, as in the conduct producing the discourse. Both cognitive and noncognitive theorists have seized upon certain aspects of moral discourse and have tried to force all the rest into the pattern dictated by this segment. Hence, each has been critical of the other and has yet remained relatively impervious to criticism, because it has seen the criticism as arising from misunderstanding. Each has been subject to a certain confusion of criteria and has defended itself by arguing that it has met those criteria which it has recognized, not seeing that the force of the criticisms indicates a need for additional criteria, or at least for clarification of criteria.

A theory which grants the variety of ethical forms and explicitly faces each of the criteria we have found necessary, will of necessity be complex. If there are a variety of forms, we must seek to ascertain the relationship they may have to each other, and how they combine or conflict in a concrete ethical situation. One result of this necessary complexity will be that we must admit problems may arise in which no clear-cut answer can be given, in which no *warranted* ethical judgment can be made. But this should not lead us to assert, as some have, that therefore *no* ethical judgments can ever be justified, or that this demonstrates that empirical facts have no logical relation to ethical judgments. Rather it only demonstrates that in *some* situations the facts do not indicate an unambiguous ethical conclusion. This surely accords with our experience; we find in many situations that the facts clearly indicate which course of action would be best and the only problem involved is one of overcoming the inertia of habit and indifference; but we also find there are other situations in which the best of wills must falter because each of the actions possible has some unwanted consequences, and none seems clearly better than some alternative.

My plan for the remainder of this study is this: in chapter IV, I shall present an analysis of judgments of evaluation. This will be concerned, as far as it is possible, only with what we may call pure judgments of evaluation, namely, judgments asserting only that some action or state of affairs is good or bad, better or worse, than alternatives, without imputing to anyone an obligation to perform any action or seek to bring about any state of affairs. Where judgments function both to assert evaluations and ascribe obligations, I shall in this chapter be concerned with them only as judgments of evaluation.

Chapter V will deal with judgments of obligation, similarly concentrating on pure judgments of this type, namely, judgments asserting the existence of obligations or duties without containing any evaluation of the acts said to be obligatory. This may seem to some to be an unwarranted abstraction, since it may be thought that all ethical judgments involve both evaluation and obligation. But one of the purposes of these chapters will be to suggest that many ordinary ethical judgments are in fact pure judgments of evaluation or of obligation, and that they must be seen as such if justification is to be possible.

In chapter VI I shall trace the relationship between evaluation and obligation and consider those judgments which combine the two functions. It is hoped that after we have analyzed the two types of judgment separately, the full complexity of moral discourse will appear in a new perspective from which it will prove more amenable to analysis.

Chapter IV

JUDGMENTS OF EVALUATION

THERE ARE TWO fundamentally different types of ethical judgment, judgments of evaluation and judgments of obligation, and any adequate ethical theory must provide analyses of both. This point has been asserted and repeated in the preceding chapters, and has been held to be of particular pertinence for any naturalistic or empiricist ethical theory, since only by constant attention to this distinction can any such theory escape the criticisms traditionally directed at it. But we have yet made no attempt to specify how one is to decide in any particular instance just which type an ethical judgment may be. Consequently, before offering an analysis of judgments of evaluation, we may do well to try to clarify further this basic distinction.

In the sense here intended, judgments of evaluation are those judgments that attribute any degree of worth, excellence, or value, positive or negative, absolute or comparative, to an actual or possible existent, to any object, situation, state of affairs, or to some *kind* of thing. Judgments of obligation are those judgments that ascribe an obligation to some person, or group or organization of persons. The difficulty experienced in distinguishing judgments of the two types has several sources: we often employ the same "ethical terms" in both types of judgment; some judgments of each type are directly normative, that is, they function by themselves to direct particular actions or, as is sometimes said, they hold an imperative for action; and many ethical judgments combine the two functions.

It is not difficult to cite clear-cut cases of each type of judgment. We may say "You have no obligation, but it would be better if you did so-and-so," and this is clearly a judgment of evaluation. Or we may say "No matter what the consequences, it is your duty to do so-and-so," and this is clearly a judgment of obligation. The occurrence of such judgments in our conversations assures us that the distinction made is a legitimate one, marked in our ordinary usage, and that we will do well to at least begin by assuming that the two types of judgment are independent. The difficulty arises with the many judgments which do not contain clauses to make the distinction for us and thus have often been taken uncritically as both "value judgments" and ascriptions of obligation. It may be that the most important step in clarifying the language of ethics is that of distinguishing these two types of judgment.

The presence of particular terms is not a sure sign of which type a judgment may be, but in some circumstances it seems a fairly reliable indication. Statements of the form "X is good" are most often judgments of evaluation, whereas, of course, the terms "obligation" and "duty" indicate judgments of obligation. The judgments that most easily lend themselves to confusion are, perhaps, those containing the term "ought." Many writers tend to regard any statement containing "ought" as a judgment of obligation, without any question; even those who distinguish several senses of "ought" often assume that all of the senses alike ascribe obligation. But we have already seen that there are at least some instances in which the result of translating "ought" into "has an obligation" is to transform a possibly true sentence into a certainly false one; hence, in some uses "ought" must be construed as "ought_e" and not as "ought_o."

Obligations are always ascribed to particular persons or groups of persons, and are always obligations to perform some particular act or kind of act or one of a set of alternative actions, each of which will probably bring about a certain state of affairs. Further, we never claim that anyone has an obligation to do anything that is not a thing of a *kind* humans are capable of doing voluntarily; that is, no act can be obligatory unless it is the sort of thing about which we can sometimes truthfully say "B can do X," where this means "B is able to do X, if he chooses," or "X will occur, if B wills it," or "B knows how to do X and is physically capable of doing it," or, in Prichard's terms, "B can set himself to bring about X, and his setting himself will then bring about something which will have X as its effect."[1]

We do sometimes claim that a person has an obligation to do something he cannot *in the circumstances* do. For example, we ordinarily hold that one has an obligation to pay a debt even though he may not now have the money and hence *cannot* now pay it. Therefore we cannot hold, without qualification, that "ought_o" implies "can" if this is taken to mean that we may have obligations only to perform acts that we are actually able to perform at the time. To assert this would imply the admission that one might borrow freely, secure in the knowledge that if he were unable to repay he would then cease to have any obligation to repay, and this is surely not in accord with our ordinary ways of thinking. In such situations we say "I cannot fulfill my obligation," not "I have no obligation."

"Ought_o" does imply "can," however, in the sense that we may only have obligations to perform acts of a *kind* humans are capable of per-

---

[1] Cf. William Frankena, "Obligation and Ability," in Max Black, ed., *Philosophical Analysis* (Ithaca: Cornell University Press, 1950), p. 158.

forming voluntarily. To say someone has an obligation is to say he is *bound* to the performance of some act, but we cannot be bound to perform acts that cannot be performed voluntarily.

On the other hand, "ought," does not imply "can" in any sense. We may say "It would be better if there were a heaven" or "It would be better if you were six inches taller," and these statements remain reasonable and possibly true when restated as "There ought to be a heaven" and "You ought to be six inches taller," even though it be admitted these are not states of affairs that can be voluntarily produced.

From these observations we may conclude that any ethical statement which does not relate a person or persons to some action of a kind which can be voluntarily performed cannot be taken as a judgment of obligation, but must rather be regarded as a judgment of evaluation. This will not suffice to allow us to make the desired distinction in every instance, but does mark off several classes of judgments as judgments of evaluation. As seen in the preceding chapter, statements describing something as "desirable" or "undesirable" fall into this category, since desiring is not an act that can be performed at will, even though we can perform actions which will lead to our having the proper desires in the future. Similarly, statements which describe feelings or emotions as "good," "right," or assert that someone ought to have them, must be taken as judgments of evaluation. In this class are such statements as "You ought to feel gratitude to a benefactor."

Statements which attribute a value to objects are also, in general, to be understood as judgments of evaluation, as are judgments which appraise persons or characters; to translate them in Stevensonian fashion into "I approve of X, kindly do so as well" does not alter this status, since approval, like desire, cannot be had at will or on order.

Statements asserting that some thing or state of affairs ought to exist are also judgments of evaluation. In this classification fall statements such as "There ought to be less disease in the world" and "There ought to be a higher standard of living in Asia."

Those statements which do relate a person or persons to some action of a kind that can be voluntarily performed are not so easily classified. I shall contend that some of these must also be understood as pure judgments of evaluation, though others may combine the two functions. The reasons for this contention cannot be specified, however, until we have inquired further into the nature of obligation. We shall then also be able to consider the question of whether our classification is not invalidated by the fact that many of the statements we have called judgments of evaluation imply statements that are undoubtedly judgments of obligation. It might be felt, for example, that "X ought$_e$ to be desired" implies "you (or someone) ought$_o$ to act so as to maintain X in existence." I shall maintain that a defensible naturalistic theory can be constructed only if it is seen that judgments containing only "ought$_e$" *cannot, by themselves,* ever imply judgments containing "ought$_o$,"[2] but the defense of this position must await the next chapter.

Even if it be admitted that some judgments of evaluation imply judgments of obligation, it would still be necessary to distinguish the two, if only in order that the relation between them be made clearer. It is evident, at least, that not *all* judgments of evaluation imply judgments of obligation; we may say of a dead man, for example, that he ought$_e$ to have lived to enjoy his son's success, but this surely cannot be taken as implying any obligation. One purpose of isolating judgments of evaluation would then be to determine how those which do imply judgments of obligation differ from those which do not. Further, even if "ought$_e$" implies "ought$_o$," we must have a method of justifying judgments of evaluation before we can assert the implied judgment of obligation. If "X is better than any alternative" implies "B ought$_o$ to do X," then we must be able to justify the former, as a pure judgment of evaluation, before we can assert the latter.

This discussion does not pretend to be a complete or even adequate treatment of the distinction between the two types of judgment. Such a treatment, if it is to be given at all, must emerge in the subsequent analyses of the two types. What I have tried to do here is only to indicate some of the kinds of statements I take to be judgments of evaluation and suggest some of the reasons why I take the distinction to be essential. It is hoped that both the distinction and the reasons will become clearer as we go on.

Throughout the remainder of this chapter I shall be concerned almost exclusively with judgments of evaluation—mostly statements containing "ought$_e$." I do not wish to contend that none of these statements may not *also* be a judgment of obligation. The reader may in some instances, when he comes upon an "ought$_e$," be impelled to exclaim "Why not 'ought$_o$,' also?" and he may be correct. The point I wish to stress, to avoid misunderstanding, is that I shall here consider these

---

[2] This contention—that "ought$_e$" does not imply "ought$_o$"—is, I believe, substantially the same as that made by C. I. Lewis in the final section of his *Analysis of Knowledge and Valuation,* though couched in somewhat different terms. The main difference, if any, lies in Lewis' narrower view of what constitutes an "ethical problem."

statements only as judgments of evaluation, ignoring their obligatory aspect, as in the next chapter I shall consider them only as judgments of obligation.

The essentials of the theory of value that will be assumed and will underlie the following discussion of judgments of evaluation have been perhaps most succinctly expressed in a sentence of John Dewey's: "There is no value except where there is satisfaction, but there have to be certain conditions fulfilled to transform a satisfaction into a value."[3]

Since it is the avowed intention of this treatise to defend an empiricist ethical theory, we must be as empirical about what is good as about what is round or red. That is, I shall accept as good what humans *find* to be good in their experience. It is a fact as objective and stubborn as any that humans in their daily living find some elements in experience to be good and others to be bad, and that these directly experienced goods and ills then serve as a basis for preference and as a guide in action. Further, when their actions are not merely impulsive or compulsive, humans, in general, direct their actions toward the goal of a good life.

These goods and evils immediately found in experience[4] are designated by a wide range of terms in our ordinary language. We speak of things, events, and our experience of them as: good, satisfying, delightful, pleasant, amusing, wonderful, superb, moving, fine, excellent, etc.; or as: bad, evil, dissatisfying, painful, annoying, dull, horrible, disgusting, poor, dreadful, etc. And we have no difficulty in communicating with these terms; statements containing them are usually neither intended nor interpreted as mere expressions of emotion, as commands, or as announcements of wholly inexplicable likings and dislikings of the speaker, but rather as reports or predictions of experiences of immediate, directly realizable value or disvalue.

Furthermore, we all assume that the directly apprehended *value qualities* permeating the content of experience are roughly the same in the experience of all men, though men may have quite different ex-

---

[3] "The Construction of Good," in Wilfrid Sellars and John Hospers, eds., *Readings in Ethical Theory* (New York: Appleton-Century-Crofts, 1952), p. 280. I believe that a fundamentally sound empirical theory of value has been set forth in the writings of Dewey and C. I. Lewis, whose work in this field I take to be complementary. I shall not here attempt any detailed exposition or defense of this theory, but rather shall accept it as defensible and attempt to show that an analysis of judgments of evaluation, interpreted in accord with the theory, can meet the proposed criteria for an adequate ethical theory.

[4] For a detailed discussion of these directly experienced values, see C. I. Lewis, *An Analysis of Knowledge and Valuation* (La Salle: Open Court, 1946), chap. xiii.

perience of the same *object* or *situation*. That is, we freely admit that things or activities we find "delightful" or "satisfying" may be found by others to be "boring" or "dissatisfying" or worse, but we seldom conclude from this that the very quality of an *experience* to which we refer in calling something "satisfying" is also referred to by the others in calling it "dissatisfying." Rather we assume that we and the others mean the same thing, designate the same directly apprehended quality, by the term "satisfying" and, in the situation in question, this quality occurs in our experience and does not occur in the experience of others.

These immediately apprehended and realized goods and ills Lewis calls the "immediately valuable," and as such they provide the empirical ground of our value statements. Without them, as Lewis says, there could be no determination of values, or of what is valuable, in any *other* sense, or any significance for value terms at all.

I shall use the term "satisfaction" to refer to those goods that may be immediately realized in experience. But it must be recognized that any one term may be misleading, since it is being called upon to cover a wide range of experience. To avoid any such misconception of the meaning intended, I can perhaps do no better than quote two passages from Lewis:

Immediate or directly findable value is not so much one quality as a dimension-like mode which is pervasive of all experience. There is not one goodness and one badness to be found in living but uncountably many variants of good and bad, each like every other most notably in being a basis for choosing and preferring. Value or disvalue is not like the pitch of middle C or the seen color of median red or the felt hardness of steel. It is not one specific quale of experience but a gamut of such; more like color in general or pitch or hardness in general.[5]

If 'pleasure' or any other name is to serve as synonym for the immediately and intrinsically valuable, then it must be adequate to the wide variety of what is found directly good in life. It must cover the active and self-forgetting satisfactions as well as the passive and self-conscious ones; the sense of integrity in firmly fronting the 'unpleasant' as well as 'pleasure'; the gratification in having one's own way, and also the benediction which may come to the defeated in having finished the faith. It must cover innocent satisfactions as well as those of cultivation; that which is found in consistency and also that of perversity and caprice; the enjoyment of sheer good fortune, and that which adds itself to dogged achievement. All this in addition to the whole range of the sensuously pleasing and the emotionally gratifying. And the immediately disvaluable has its equal and corresponding variety. Such immediate goods and bads are ill compressed into any term or pair of them.... We do better to call upon our pervasive sense of this mode of all experience, and the multiplicity of its modalities, to correct any chosen name, than we should in depending on the name to conjure up the requisite inclusive sense of the possible goods of life. The variety of our adjectives of prizing is better taken as indicative than would be any one of them; which might well be too narrow.[6]

[5] *Ibid.*, p. 401.   [6] *Ibid.*, p. 405.

I shall mean by "satisfaction," then, any such experience of immediate value. Empiricist value theories have not always taken these directly experienced goods as fundamental, but have instead asserted the basic value concept to be "object of interest (or desire)" or "realization of objects of interest (or desire)." The reason for taking satisfactions as basic over these alternatives, is, as Henry Aiken has said, empirical.[7] Objects of interest often do lead to an experienced goodness, and the realization of an object of interest is often a satisfaction, but this is not inevitably so.

It seems unwise to propose as an empirical theory one committed by its basic category to defend as "good," just because they happen to arouse interest or desire, things that are when experienced rejected as "bad." If all of our desires and interests were intelligently formed and based upon sufficient experience, this would perhaps be an unimportant point. But not only children are attracted by fancy names or the gleam of a shiny object, and vociferously demand to have foods they have never tasted and objects but obscurely apprehended; this characteristic we all only slowly, if ever, overcome. And it is a characteristic not to be lightly condemned, for without it we should pass by many an undiscovered good and deprive ourselves of much of the varied richness of the world.

My contention is not that we should renounce the attraction of all the small glitterings that catch our eye, but that such attractions do not infallibly indicate that the glittering object when had will be experienced as good. As Aiken has said, "The occurrence of satisfactions is dependent in the last analysis not upon achieving results that we think we want, but upon actualizing consummatory behavior patterns which, in many instances, occur without any preparatory or anticipatory activity whatever."[8]

The view I am advocating rests upon the fact that we, that humans in general, do find some portions of our experience to be immediately good and some to be immediately bad, and the qualities of experience to which we refer by such terms as "satisfying," "enjoyable," "pleasant," "painful," "annoying," are generally assumed to be common to us all, to occur in the experience of all normal humans, though not necessarily in experience of the same objects or situations. It is, however, a fact equally objective and stubborn that humans also inevitably find that some directly experienced goods are not good in the long run, since they either lead to evils or stand in the way of further goods, and some experienced evils are not evil in the long run, since they either

[7] "Evaluation and Obligation," *Journal of Philosophy*, XLVII (1950), 8.
[8] *Ibid.*

lead to goods or prevent further evils. Hence the final value of any particular experience or thing experienced cannot be gauged solely in terms of its own presented content, but rather can be judged only when this experience or object is seen in relation to a larger whole of experience of which it is a part. If we learn anything from experience, it is this. The testimony accumulated through the ages confirms it. We express this knowledge in proverb and song, in legend and myth, and in the stories we tell our children. It is the beginning of wisdom.

This inescapable fact makes necessary the second part of Dewey's statement: There have to be certain conditions fulfilled to transform a satisfaction into a value. For while we do in fact regard such directly realized goods as "intrinsically good," in the sense of "good for its own sake," this is by no means to say that we consider them above criticism, or feel that any particular experienced good or evil must be accepted in its own terms as a final value or disvalue.

As Dewey uses the term, only that is a "value" which is "worth having" or which it would be rational to desire; but any particular satisfaction, or object providing a satisfaction, cannot be granted such status without further inquiry. These satisfactions do not occur in isolation from the rest of experience, and it is only when they are seen and weighed in all of their connections and relations with the means that bring them about and the further ends to which they are means that they become subjects for warranted judgments of evaluation. The goods we find in living are indeed goods, but no one of them can be deemed a *value,* in Dewey's sense, until it is known in its connections with other things and further experience. In the words of C. I. Lewis: "... if in one sense the determination of values must be eventually in terms of the value qualities of direct experience, still in another sense no immediately experienced good or bad is final, but rather is further to be evaluated by its relation to the temporal whole of a good life."[9]

This disparity between immediately realized goods and the final evaluation of such goods has led both Dewey and Lewis to insist on a distinction they assert to be essential for any empirical theory of evaluation: the distinction, that is, between those statements which merely report the occurrence of immediately experienced goods and evils, and those statements which ascribe *value* to an object, a situation, a state of affairs, or to some kind of thing.

Statements that are mere reports of the presented content of immediate experience are not, both Dewey and Lewis insist, *judgments* at all. We usually do not consider they require verification; in Dewey's

[9] *Op. cit.,* p. 483.

words, they are "just correct or incorrect and that is the end of the matter."[10] As Lewis states (and Dewey agrees), "the apprehension expressed is not a judgment, and is not to be classed as knowledge."[11]

We must also note that these reports are not normative. Such reports do sometimes contain the terms "good" or "right" and may even be indistinguishable in appearance from normative judgments of evaluation, but if the statement is intended and understood as merely a report of the character of the presented content of experience, then it is neither felt as authoritative in any way nor functions directively.

Our behavior may be influenced by such reports, of course. Hearing someone say that a particular food tastes good, we may assume that we would also find it good and so be motivated to taste it. But the report that it tastes good does not direct us to taste it nor assert that if we tasted it, we would find it good—to take the report as having any such content is to interpret it not as a report but as a judgment of evaluation. Where reports of immediate value experiences are concerned, there is no question of justifying the report or accounting for any normative character; to raise such a question is to mistake the report for a judgment of evaluation.

The occurrence of immediate felt qualities of goodness and badness and of statements reporting these occurrences, creates rather than solves problems of evaluation—problems of how these particular satisfactions or dissatisfactions are to be rated in the wider context of our continuing personal and communal life. The problems thus raised can be solved only by recourse to a process of evaluation. From this process of reflection and inquiry issue statements attributing an objective value to an existent or possible existent. As such the statements *are* judgments and do constitute knowledge. In terms Dewey has often repeated, they judge that something is enjoyable, desirable, or satisfactory, as compared to enjoyed, desired, or satisfying. It is of course true that not all statements intended to ascribe objective value are based upon reflection and inquiry; many, we must admit, have no basis other than superstition, dogma, or wishful thinking. But a central doctrine in the theory of Dewey and Lewis is the contention that such judgments are warranted assertions only when they do issue from inquiry and reflection.

Statements of this latter sort, those by which we intend to ascribe objective value, constitute the judgments of evaluation that demand analysis. Mere reports of experienced good or ill are not judgments at

[10] "The Construction of Good," in Sellars and Hospers, *op. cit.*, p. 275.
[11] *Op. cit.*, p. 375.

all, though the experiences so reported are, in a sense, ultimate for an empirical theory of evaluation, since any judgment of evaluation can only be justified by reference to such experiences. No one satisfaction allows us to say of a state of affairs that it is satisfactory, but that it *is* satisfactory can only be established by way of the satisfactions to which it gives rise.

Judgments of evaluation, if they are to be empirical, must refer ultimately to goods or evils directly realized in experience—to satisfactions. We may not justifiably call an object "valuable," for example, unless it may in some way be instrumental to a directly experienced good. The reference to experiences of immediate value is in many instances indirect, an object being instrumental to some further object which may also be only instrumental, etc., but unless some such series of connections can be traced from the original object to an experienced goodness, we are not warranted in asserting that it is valuable.

Though they must all finally refer to satisfactions and all be distinguished from mere reports of occurrent immediate value, judgments of evaluation are not therefore homogeneous. Several important distinctions must be made among them. The major types as classified by Lewis[12] are: judgments of *inherent value,* judgments of *instrumental value,* and judgments of *contributory value.* Objects may have either inherent or instrumental value: the presence of the object itself may be the immediate occasion of satisfaction or dissatisfaction, as when we experience a picture as beautiful or ugly; or the object may merely be causally connected (instrumental) to the presentation of some *other* object which has inherent value, as a bus may be instrumental in transporting us to the museum.

Judgments of contributory value are, on the other hand, evaluations of values, judgments as to the worth of having particular satisfactions, of pursuing particular goods as ends when these are viewed in their relation to a larger whole of experience. As such they are the judgments of evaluation with which ethics is most immediately concerned. These are also the judgments most challenging to empiricists, since they most markedly have the normative or *de jure* quality that critics claim eludes any naturalistic analysis.

Cutting across this classification of types of judgment is another distinction of some importance, that between statements ascribing value relative to the experience of a single person, usually the speaker or hearer, and those ascribing value relative to a group of persons. We may call these respectively *personal* and *interpersonal* value ascrip-

[12] *Op. cit.,* p. 391.

tions. Statements of any of the types mentioned may be intended to refer to the experience either of one particular person or to all or most persons in a particular group. The size of the group may range from two to all of mankind. All value statements must be either personal or interpersonal value ascriptions.

I have tried here to set forth briefly the empirical foundation of the theory to be offered and to provide a classification of types of value statement. Human experience is permeated with immediately apprehended goods and evils—satisfactions and dissatisfactions. These experiences of immediate value provide the empirical basis for our judgments of evaluation. Any judgment of evaluation, if it is to be empirical, must refer ultimately to some such experience. Insofar as judgments of evaluation derive from, refer to, and predict experiences of immediate value, they have a testable empirical content and share with other empirical statements the characteristics of being fallible, corrigible, and only probable.

On the basis of this discussion, we may now turn more directly to the task of analyzing judgments of evaluation.

Evaluations become necessary when problems beset us, when action is blocked and several paths seem open for its renewal, when doubts arise as to accepted ends, when competing alternatives each attract or each repel with seeming equal strength.

All evaluations, and all judgments of evaluation, take place in the context of an on-going life process immersed in an interconnected world of persons acting in and in relation to an environment. Every judgment of evaluation is arrived at and expressed by a person whose experience of the world has been to a degree moulded by his upbringing in a particular community at a particular time, who is not only a self-conscious individual, but also is or has been a member of a number of overlapping groups or communities and has had built into his character structure some of the attitudes of these communities. Value problems, and hence evaluations, occur only in the experience of humans who have internalized their past and carry it everywhere with them, and envision a future conceived as an orderly development out of this past; those objects and states of affairs that have been experienced as good in the past are in general expected to prove good in the future; those rules of conduct that have been successful in the past are in general expected to prove successful in the future.

These facts are not merely accidental and unimportant to the process of evaluation or to an analysis of evaluation. Rather they are constitutive of the process and must be heeded in any analysis. It is not unimportant that it is persons who make evaluations and that all evaluations take place within and with reference to a wider context of personal and community life. And it is not accidental that each person brings to every value problem some of the attitudes of the community. As George Herbert Mead has shown, the development of the self takes place only as the individual puts himself in the role of others, takes over the responses and attitudes of the other, puts himself "in the place of the generalized other, which represents the organized responses of all of the members of the group." Mead writes:

What goes to make up the organized self is the organization of the attitudes which are common to the group. A person is a personality because he belongs to a community, because he takes over the institutions of that community into his own conduct. He takes its language as a medium by which he gets his personality, and then through a process of taking the different roles that all the others furnish he comes to get the attitude of the members of the community. Such, in a certain sense, is the structure of a man's personality. There are certain common responses which each individual has toward certain common things, and in so far as those common responses are awakened in the individual when he is affecting other persons he arouses his own self. The structure, then, on which the self is built is this response which is common to all, for one has to be a member of a community to be a self.[13]

The facts I wish to stress are these: evaluations are called forth in the context of particular problems. These problems are not isolated but themselves arise in the midst of a continuing active life. The person who finds himself involved in a value-problem and then undertakes a process of evaluation, brings to this process his experience of the past, his hopes for the future, and the internalized attitudes and responses of the communities of which he is a member. Thus every evaluation takes place in a context of acknowledged ends or goals[14] and of accepted regulative principles believed instrumental to these goals. And at least some, and usually all, of these goals and principles are shared, or believed to be shared, by the members of a community. Any one of these acknowledged ends or accepted regulative principles may be challenged and itself subjected to a process of evaluation, but in this process itself some ends will be acknowledged and some principles accepted.

These facts are essential for any understanding and analysis of judgments of evaluation. Two aspects are of crucial importance: the significance of the individual's membership in a community and the role of acknowledged ends and accepted regulative principles. If these factors are not admitted as relevant in every context of evaluation, then the

---

[13] *Mind, Self and Society* (Chicago: University of Chicago Press, 1934), p. 162.

[14] I use "ends or goals" here in a sense intended to include what is to be avoided as well as what is to be sought.

function and justification of judgments of evaluation becomes as mysterious and inexplicable as some philosophers have made it out to be. On the other hand, if their existence and relevance is admitted, then it can be seen how judgments of evaluation may be both normative and empirically justifiable.

It will be recalled that the three criteria an analysis of judgments of evaluation must meet are: (1) it must provide for a ground for the judgment; (2) it must account for the felt motivational force of the judgment; and (3) it must provide for a warrant for the judgment. Though the structure of the analysis remains roughly the same throughout, the various types of judgments of evaluation exhibit differences significant enough to warrant discussing them separately.

The judgments of evaluation most easily dealt with are those ascribing *personal* instrumental or inherent value, that is, judgments attributing instrumental or inherent value to an existent or possible existent relative to the experience of a single person only, whom I shall call A. Such judgments frequently occur in contexts varying from those of choosing a gift for a friend or a book to read to choosing a career.

A judgment of personal *instrumental* value, which may be asserted as "X is good (for A)," is *grounded* in empirical knowledge or matter-of-fact propositions when a number of such propositions is adduced sufficient to establish the probability that the object or action in question will be instrumental to some directly realized good, some satisfaction, in the experience of A or will lead to some end acknowledged as an end by A.

These factual statements will in most instances assert the existence of causal connections, or will testify that the same or similar objects or actions have in similar circumstances in the past led to such satisfactions or ends for A, or for persons who are similar to A in relevant respects.

Similarly, judgments of personal *inherent* value are grounded in empirical knowledge when a number of empirical statements are adduced sufficient to establish the probability that, under normal conditions, or under the particular conditions which prevail, A will find satisfaction in direct experience of the object judged good.

All judgments of personal instrumental or inherent value may, in a sense, be said to be prescriptive; they describe certain objects or actions as valuable for A, whoever A may be, and thus prescribe or perhaps recommend that A cherish these objects or perform these actions. But these judgments are not all felt as authoritative in the context of their occurrence. For A may not be present when the judgment is uttered—

he need not even be alive—and neither the speaker nor hearer may feel at all urged or motivated to act in A's interest. Nevertheless, many such judgments do have a felt authority, a normative force, when uttered. This is so when A is either the speaker or hearer, or when the speaker or hearer is so related to A as to have taken over, at least momentarily, his attitudes.

This normative force cannot, I believe, be related simply to one source, such as "emotive meaning," but has several possible sources, one or more of which may be operative in any particular situation. By noting the multiple source such felt authority may have, we can account for the normative character of the many different sorts of judgment of evaluation as well as of judgments of obligation without attempting to reduce them all to the same "pattern of analysis."

One major source of the normative power of judgments of inherent or instrumental value lies in the attraction of the anticipated satisfactions or acknowledged goals to which the object or action is reputed to lead. When we call any object or action "good" or "valuable" for someone, or say he "ought$_e$" to do something, meaning by this that the object or action will lead to satisfactions for him or provide more satisfactions than some alternative, we expect that he will then feel motivated toward these satisfactions. And this is not an unreasonable expectation.

Under normal conditions normal humans will feel motivated to reinstate as goals those objects that in the past have provided satisfactions, and to install as goals those objects that promise to provide satisfactions in the future. This means that "among healthy organisms, not acting under stress, empirically tested evaluations will tend to have some normative appeal or urgency."[15] Similarly, acknowledged goals and their means have a normative appeal; to acknowledge a goal is to accept it *as a goal*, and this involves motivation not only toward the goal but toward the means to the goal.

We may note here that in this aspect the normative force of these judgments of evaluation is not the force of compulsion but rather of attraction. Even when the object or action in question is not one we have previously desired, the force of the judgment of evaluation is not such as to compel us to do something against our wills or desires, but rather to present the object as desirable, as an object we would desire if we saw things clearly.

A second factor in creating the felt normative force of a judgment lies in the compulsion of the situation or the problem in which the evaluation takes place. We usually undertake evaluations only in con-

---

[15] Henry Aiken, "Evaluation and Obligation," *Journal of Philosophy*, XLVII (1950), 15.

texts in which we are from the beginning committed to choose some alternative or take some action. We may be choosing a picture for a particular room, a book for Aunt Sarah, a doctor for a sick child, or deciding whether to go to college or accept a job, or which college to go to, or which candidate to vote for; in all such instances the felt *need* to do *something* becomes transformed into the felt *compulsion* to do *this thing,* when this thing emerges from the process of evaluation as "good" or "the best." A felt normative force is imparted to the judgment of evaluation by the felt necessity inherent in the situation.

The language employed in expressing the judgment functions as a third source. We may here take account of all that the noncognitivists have said about the "emotive," "persuasive," "dynamic," "instrumental" qualities of ethical language, of the effects of intonation and gesture, and of the similarities which Margaret MacDonald has noted between ethical language and the language of ritual and ceremony. But to say that a statement has these characteristics is by no means ground for attributing to it some new kind of "meaning" setting it off from "scientific" language—most of these characteristics may be found in the language of scientists as well as in ethical discourse, and in no way restrict the cognitive content of the statement. Further, I feel this is only a secondary source of the normative force of judgments of evaluation, and would not continue long to be effective if it were not continually reinforced by our experiencing as good those things said to be "good."

A fourth source which may be mentioned is the authority of the speaker. If the speaker is respected or looked to for guidance, or is in a position of authority or command, his words are lent a force that would be lacking when spoken by another.

It seems probable that in some instances the total normative force of a judgment of evaluation may derive from the third and fourth sources. Someone may, that is, be quite unmindful of the necessity of the situation and unmoved by the goals prescribed, yet be motivated to action by the mere force of the language employed and the authority imparted to it by the speaker. This possibility is one we must view with mixed feelings, for it may have both good and evil consequences. It may, on the one hand, lead to the pursuit of genuinely good goals or the performance of genuinely good actions by one who would not otherwise so act; but on the other hand, it may also lead to the blind pursuit of ends dictated by a demagogue, or the undertaking of actions whose import is not at all understood and which may be largely destructive.

We have so far discussed the *ground* and the *normative force* of judgments of personal instrumental or inherent value, although some of the remarks made apply beyond these to judgments of evaluation in general. We may now turn to the question of the justification of these judgments of personal value, to the task of providing a *warrant* for them. The discussion of this criterion in the preceding chapter disclosed that this requires that not only the cognitive content of the judgment be justified, but also its normative force. It must be shown, that is, that it is reasonable to accept the judgment as a directive and to be directed by it.

In many contexts value statements occur merely as predictions of future satisfactions. In judgments of personal value, the prediction is either that A will have an experience of immediate value or disvalue under certain conditions, or that a particular object (or kind of object) will be instrumental to (or provide) satisfactions for A *whenever* certain specifiable conditions occur. Predictions of the first sort are, in Lewis' terms, "terminating judgments," verifiable by the single occurrence or failure of occurrence of the predicted satisfaction; those of the second sort are not at any given time completely verified, but are confirmed to some degree or made probable by the occurrence or nonoccurrence of satisfactions under the proper conditions.[16]

Value statements of each of these types are, as Lewis has shown, empirical statements and are verifiable by the same general methods as are any other empirical statements. But we must here join the critics of crude naturalistic ethical theories in insisting that such verification does not, in itself, justify the normative force such statements may have; it does not show that it is reasonable to accept them as directive. For, even though the predicted satisfactions do occur, they may be satisfactions that it is not reasonable to seek. It may be true that X is good, when this is meant only to assert that X will lead to some satisfactions for A, and yet be false that A ought, to do X, when this is meant to assert that it would better if A did X.

This situation may seem to be one in which verification of the reputed cognitive content of a value statement does not suffice to justify it as a value statement; hence, it may seem to confirm the noncognitivist contention that all value statements are incapable of cognitive justification. But closer inspection reveals this as one of the many instances in which the ambiguity of our ordinary value-language creates difficulty. The difficulty here is a confusion over the actual cognitive content of the statement. If the statement is intended and interpreted as

---

[16] Cf. Lewis, *op. cit.*, p. 375.

51

merely a prediction of particular satisfactions for A, then it is indeed verifiable by the occurrence of these satisfactions. But this is the end of it; for the assertion "X is good" is then no more normative than would be the assertion that particular satisfactions will occur—it no more asserts that A ought₈ seek these satisfactions than does the simple prediction.

We are involved in a logical confusion if we intend or interpret a statement both as a normative ethical statement and as a mere prediction of satisfactions, for, *by meaning or interpreting the statement as normative, we give it a wider cognitive content than the mere prediction.* The content it has *as normative* is not only "X will lead to satisfactions for A" but also "these satisfactions are *worth having.*"

The justification or warrant of judgments of evaluation demanded by our criterion is a justification of the judgment as normative;[17] hence this justification must be more complex than mere verification of the probable occurrence of predicted satisfactions. Such verification is only the first step in warranting the judgment; beyond this is required a warrant for the predicted satisfactions or the acknowledged goals to which the object is instrumental. This second step involves the justification of a judgment of *contributory* value, an evaluation of a particular value. The details of this process will be discussed in the following analysis of judgments of this type. The point to be made here is that the justification of any *normative* judgment of instrumental or inherent value requires the justification of a judgment of contributory value.

The process of providing a warrant for judgments of personal instrumental or inherent value, then, involves the following steps: (1) It must be established that the empirical reasons offered as a ground for the statement are in fact sufficient as a ground; the reasons, if true, must be sufficient to establish the probability that the object or action judged will be instrumental to or provide the stated satisfactions or the acknowledged goals. (2) These reasons must be verified as true or highly probable. (3) The satisfactions or the acknowledged goals must themselves be warranted.

Unlike the simple verification of predicted satisfactions, this form of justification both warrants the asserted cognitive content of the judgment and, in doing so, justifies its normative force. Part of the asserted content is that these satisfactions or goals are worthy of being

---

[17] If, as is often true, an appraisal is not normative, but merely asserts that a particular instrument will be good for reaching a particular end, then mere verification of the instrument's efficiency suffices to justify the assertion. The empirical status of this sort of statement has seldom been questioned.

pursued; and one, if not the only, method of justifying a directive to undertake actions leading to particular ends is by certifying these ends as worthy of pursuit. A major source of the felt normative force of these judgments is the desire for and anticipation of the promised satisfactions or goals, and the establishment of these goals as warranted not only confirms the desire as reasonable, but also justifies the acceptance of the judgment as directive.

We must now turn to a consideration of judgments of personal contributory value. These judgments have emerged as central in the analysis; if they cannot be justified, then *no* normative judgment of personal value may be warranted. The justification of judgments of instrumental or inherent value presupposes the justification of judgments of contributory value.

But this is not the only relation between these types of judgment. Problems of the evaluation of ends do not ordinarily arise apart from problems of the evaluation of means—judgments of instrumental or inherent value—and, as Dewey has so often insisted, the value of ends cannot be determined without a consideration of means.

We usually act with reference to a number of projected ends of varying degrees of inclusiveness; the ends of particular actions, and hence the actions themselves, are justified by reference to the more inclusive or general ends we acknowledge. These more general ends are more often than not ends chosen for us by the community. They are ends generally acknowledged as ends in the community and we take them over as our own—this incorporation of community values into our own thought and behavior being an essential element in our membership in the community. As acknowledged general ends they function to justify more specific subordinate ends; in the context of our ordinary day-to-day living they do not receive but provide justification.

Questions of the validity of these general ends sometimes arise when the means to these ends seem in conflict with other ends we may have. Every means to a particular end has consequences other than and beyond the achieving of this end, and often these consequences may be such as to create doubts over whether the end sought is worth seeking *at this price*. When this question arises, evaluation of an end is required. But we do not carry on this evaluation simply by attending to the end itself and asking, with G. E. Moore, whether it would be a good thing if that state of affairs should exist, even if nothing else were to exist besides, either at the same time or afterward.[18] In fact,

[18] See G. E. Moore, *Ethics* (London: Oxford University Press; 1912), p. 101.

as far as I can see, this question need never enter into consideration at all. We ask rather: Given what knowledge is now available of what has existed before and what will probably exist at any time in the future, is this end worth pursuing? The need for evaluation of an end arises in a context in which means and other ends are already recognized as relevant factors, and the evaluation itself can proceed only with reference to these factors.

Those philosophers who contend that in any such process of evaluation we must eventually come to some end that is not itself justifiable, and therefore all value judgments must be considered as noncognitive, show by this contention they misunderstand the evaluation process. The process as they seem to envision it, is a linear one in which each end is justified by some further end to which it is a means—a process in which we always must have some goal left, at the end of the line, unjustified. But this is not the situation at all. Rather, we start with a set of ends, each end already certified by experience as good for its own sake, each already experienced by some humans as satisfying. If we could pursue all of these ends without any conflicts arising, then the only value questions which might beset us would be questions of the most efficient means of achieving these ends. But in our experience conflicts do arise, the pursuit of one end interferes with the pursuit of another. We then ask: Given these conditions, which ends ought₀ I pursue; which are worthy of pursuit? An answer to this question is reached by evaluating each of the ends in terms of its relations to the others—but this is not a linear process and no end need be left unevaluated. Nor is the process of evaluation a circular one, in any sense in which this would vitiate the resulting judgment of evaluation. Though each end is indeed evaluated in terms of the further ends to which it leads, or with which it conflicts, in no instance does the value of an end consist *only* in its instrumentality; each end retains its own intrinsic value.

If anything here is ultimate, it is not a particular end but the general goal of a good life, an organization of means and ends into a whole of a life that is good in the living. But the relation of particular ends to this general goal is not that of instrument to end; it is not a causal relation. Rather the good life is constituted by the organization of these more specific ends. Nor do the particular ends derive their value from this goal, as the value, say, of a violin derives from the value of the music that may be produced with it; rather the specific ends *contribute* their value to the value of the whole. To say that they are evaluated in terms of the whole is not to say that the whole is the source of their value, but rather that the reason for choosing one end over another competing end is that it contributes more to the whole.[19]

It is by this process of evaluation that we justify a judgment of contributory value. Thus it may be seen that for judgments of contributory value the distinction between *ground* and *warrant* collapses. We can provide no sufficient ground for the judgment which is not also a warrant for the judgment, as must be done for judgments of inherent or instrumental value. The content of a judgment of personal contributory value is that for A some end is worthy of pursuit. The facts upon which such a judgment may be grounded are facts concerning the needs, desires, and impulses A has and the means and probable consequences of satisfying these needs and desires. But it is by appeal to these same facts that the judgment is warranted. For the judgment that a particular goal is *desirable* or *worth seeking* is warranted when from this empirical knowledge we may infer that seeking this particular goal will probably satisfy rather than frustrate the whole organism over the long run—that it will contribute more to the goodness of a whole life than will any known alternative.[20] Such judgments, when arrived at in this fashion, are, like all empirical statements, amenable to further confirmation or correction by future experience.

The apparent difficulty of projecting events far enough into the future to be able to judge the effect of a particular action on the whole of a life is somewhat mitigated by the circumstances in which evaluations take place. Very rarely, if ever, do we select one particular goal and set out just to consider the desirability of it. Rather, since problems of evaluation originate in situations of conflict between goals, we evaluate particular goals in comparison with others. We but seldom conclude that some goal has some absolute worth—if that phrase can be given any meaning at all—but rather that some goal is better than any alternative in these circumstances. We are often able to make such comparative judgments with a rather high degree of probability, based not only on our own experience but on the accumulated evidence of

---

[19] I do not wish to suggest that the goodness of a whole or experience can be computed by simply adding up the particular satisfactions it contains. To say that a particular end contributes more to the whole than an alternative is to say that the whole is better with it than with the alternative; and this can be determined only by a consideration of the whole, and not merely by comparing the satisfactions afforded by each alternative considered alone. Cf. Lewis, *op. cit.*, pp. 488 ff.

[20] C. I. Lewis has discussed at length the details and difficulties of carrying through such an evaluation: *op. cit.*, chap. xvi, *especially* pp. 488 ff. I shall not repeat Lewis' discussion here, but refer the reader to it if he doubts the feasibility of such evaluations.

the results of many such judgments made by others. Further, we usually judge the contribution of any particular end to the whole of life in terms of its contribution to some major component of this life—a good home, a good job, a congenial community—relying on the probability that what will most contribute to the goodness of this component will also contribute most to the whole of life.

Throughout this discussion I have constantly employed the phrase "satisfactions or acknowledged goals" instead of using either term alone, and this may have seemed redundant. It is not, however; our acknowledged goals are not always states of affairs which are themselves experienced as felt satisfactions or which themselves cause later satisfactions. They may instead be conditions under which satisfactions are possible or more likely to accrue, and dissatisfactions are likely to be avoided. We are often much surer of the desirability of creating such conditions than we are of the goodness of any particular satisfaction that may accrue. Health, for example, is such an acknowledged goal. Merely being healthy is not usually itself a source of satisfaction, unless we have just recovered from an illness, but it is a condition under which we may maximize the many satisfactions of living. We realize that a healthy man may nevertheless lead a life of dull dissatisfaction and a sick man may find life supremely worth living, but our unshaken acknowledgment of health as a goal rests on the probability that in any given circumstances a healthy man will find more satisfactions than an unhealthy one and contribute more to the satisfaction of those around him.

The felt normative force of judgments of personal contributory value derives from much the same sources as does that of judgments of instrumental or inherent value; hence it is not necessary to add much to what has already been said in relation to those types of judgment. As Lewis writes: To be rational, instead of foolish or perverse, means to be capable of constraint by prevision of some future good or ill; to be amenable to the consideration "You will be sorry if you don't" or "...if you do."[21] When we are acting rationally, our present actions and decisions are imbued with a concern for the future. A felt imperative force is lent to judgments of contributory value by this concern for the future, by our desire that the future be as good as possible. A judgment of contributory value asserting some end to be desirable promises that pursuit of this end will tend to assure the desired future.

Though both judgments of contributory value and judgments of

---

[21] *Ibid.*, p. 480.

instrumental value are normative, they function in a somewhat different manner. Judgments of contributory value assert the worth of an end or acknowledged goal and so direct the hearer to seek this goal. But they are no more explicit than that, and hence do not usually by themselves direct any specific action. Rather they promote an attitude of attachment to this end rather than that, of favoring this rather than that, which will result in a difference in action only when a choice arises between actions or objects that are means to these ends. The judgment of instrumental value, on the other hand, is directly concerned with the context of choice between alternative means and does direct a specific action: "Do *this*," it directs, or "Cherish *this* object."

The relation between the two sorts of judgment in their normative function is very similar to the relation of their cognitive contents. We have seen that the attempt to justify a judgment of instrumental value discloses that such judgments contain as an implicit component a judgment of contributory value. Similarly, the normative force of the judgment of instrumental value contains as an implicit component the normative appeal of the end asserted to be good in the judgment of contributory value. In its cognitive function the judgment of instrumental value depends upon the judgment of contributory value for completion of its justification; in its normative function the judgment of instrumental value depends upon the judgment of contributory value for much of its force. The dynamic function of the judgment of contributory value is to reinforce the authority of the judgment of instrumental value.

We may now turn from judgments of personal value to judgments of interpersonal value, recognizing that much of what has already been said applies as well to either.

In the view presented here, all values are values for some living creatures, and their realization as values is relative to the conditions under which these creatures exist. All judgments of evaluation ascribe value to some existent or possible existent relative to the experience or possible experience of some living creatures. Judgments of interpersonal value are those judgments that ascribe value relative to a group of persons. A group of persons is any aggregate of persons which may be the referent of a judgment. We may refer thus to any combination or permutation of humans, living, dead, or not yet born, but usually our references are to aggregates whose members have some significant property in common—music lovers, residents of Wyoming, immigrants, octogenarians, workers, etc.

Among the many sorts of groups, the one of essential importance for a theory of evaluation is the community. A *community* of persons is an organization of persons sharing some common concerns and interests, and undertaking consciously coöperative action to attain common goals—a group in which the members recognize themselves and the others as members seeking common ends and *subject to the same restraints*. A community usually continues to exist and to maintain its identity as a community even though its membership changes. Individuals come and go, live and die, perhaps, but the community persists as long as there is a continuity of purposeful coöperative behavior and an awareness of interrelationship and interdependence among the individual members. A person may be, of course, and almost always is, a member of a number of communities at the same time. Almost all judgments of evaluation refer in some way to the values of a community; many of the most difficult and most consequential judgments we are called upon to make are judgments ascribing value relative to a community.

We may make judgments with respect to either actual or ideal communities, the latter by considering a group of persons as a community even though the members do not actually recognize themselves as such or function as such. We may then judge what would be desirable *if* such a community were actual, usually seeking through these judgments to help bring about the actuality of the community by persuading some of its potential members to think and act as members. Thus we speak often of the whole of mankind as a community even though it surely does not now function as such.

I have discussed judgments of personal and interpersonal value separately purely for purposes of analysis. In practice they are closely interconnected, so much so that a consideration of almost any judgment of either sort will turn out to involve judgments of the other. This seems fairly obvious for judgments ascribing value relative to a group, since any judgment asserting something to be good for a group can hardly be arrived at without some attention to what is good for the individuals in that group. But it is equally true that most judgments of what is good for an individual involve consideration of what is good for the communities in which he functions as a member— family, church, club, profession, union, political party, city, nation.

We are usually so deeply involved in community life that our character and personality is largely made up of attitudes and responses shared with the rest of the community. We adopt the goals of the community as our own; we feel joy in its success and sorrow for its failures. In short, we identify ourselves with the community. Our greatest satisfactions come from the part we play in the achievement of community goals; a personal triumph loses its savor if it turns out to conflict with the aims of the community, whereas experiences that would otherwise be rejected and avoided are experienced as satisfying when it is known that they forward the ends of the community. Any thorough inquiry into "my good" or "his good" must include some reference to community goods, to "our good."

I do not wish to claim that conflicts may not arise between the good of the individual and the goals of the community, for this surely does happen. An acknowledged particular goal of the community may conflict with some acknowledged particular goal of the individual, or the professed goals of the community may almost completely lose contact with the welfare of individuals, as sometimes happens when communities cling to traditional goals even though conditions have completely changed, or when the group is manipulated by some individual or subgroup without regard for the individuals in it. Conflict may also arise among the goals of the different communities to which an individual belongs.

The problem of the resolution of these conflicts will engage us in chapter VI. I may here merely note the obvious fact that for any ethics which takes as good the satisfactions experienced by individuals and yet recognizes the degree to which individuals are implicated in community life, the situations that must be viewed as most conducive to good and thus ought. be promoted are those in which the goals of the community and of the individual are in harmony, in that the goals of the community are such as to promote the welfare of its individual members.

Having said this, however, we must add that the goals of a community cannot be conceived merely in terms of maximizing any satisfactions any of its members may seek. One of the goals of any community is its continuing existence and stability as a community, its survival as a community. Thus it cannot seek to promote individual satisfactions that will be detrimental to the goal of community survival, and indeed may often restrict individual activities in the interest of community goals. A condition of the stability and survival of the community and maintenance of its identity as a community is that the members *respect* each other as members of the same community, seeking common goals and, in a way, sharing the same fate. Hence, when one member willfully injures another, this is an injury not only to the individual but also to the community.

The justification for restriction of the individual by the community must be that in general and in the long run the effects of the restriction are beneficial to the members of the community, but this question must be contested and argued in each particular case if the community goals are to remain in harmony with the individual's good. The relation between individual and community goals is reciprocal: the individual member takes over the goals of the community but he may also seek to change the goals of the community—persuade the community to adopt new goals he proposes for it. As Mead says, this is the way that society gets ahead.[22]

We are all of us members of a number of overlapping communities, ranging from family or friends to all of mankind, and we tend, at least in our use of language, to extend the range of the values we share with any one of these groups to all of them. The size of a group to which a judgment of interpersonal value refers may vary from "we two" or "those two" to "we humans" or even "we sentient creatures." Many of the difficulties arising in discussions of values relate to our frequent failure to specify the intended range of the judgment. We tend to make a general assertion "This is good" rather than say "This is good for group I." What we may be justifiably able to assert is that given the complex context which includes group I, this object or this course of action will probably contribute to a good life for the members of group I. But when we merely assert "This is good," we seem to be overlooking all of these necessary qualifications.

We seek to justify this generality by claiming that what *is* objectively valuable for group I *is* objectively valuable; but although this may be true, it may also mislead us into mistakenly expecting persons outside of the group to find value in the object or action in question. Or we defend the generality of our assertion by claiming that although the object in question is actually enjoyed only by a small group, it is potentially enjoyable to all of a larger group, perhaps all mankind, who need only the proper training and experience to enjoy it. This sort of claim may also be true in many instances, but it is rather difficult to verify.

The relativity of value judgments to particular groups or communities is most evident in aesthetic judgments, a type of judgment of interpersonal inherent value. We do not usually expect persons from a different culture, or even all from our own culture, to appreciate all our art, as we often do not appreciate theirs. But this does not restrain us from judging art objects on a scale of objective value. And there

[22] *Mind, Self and Society*, p. 168.

need be no error in this if it be recognized that though the value is objective, it remains relative to a particular group or particular conditions.

We may make judgments of interpersonal inherent value on the basis of our knowledge of the characteristics of objects the group in question has found valuable in the past, tempered by our knowledge of differences between the contemporary group and those of the past. Such judgments involve a prediction that, under suitable conditions, all or some of the group will find satisfaction in experience of the object or state of affairs in question. In reference to aesthetic judgments, this must be amended to read "all or some of the group will continue to find satisfaction in experiences of the object over a period of time," and the experience of those members who have special competence in the field must be allowed more weight than that of the rest of the group. Here, too, we infer that an object found good by the competent critics of the group would be found valuable by members of the group in general if they had the required training and experience.

Judgments of interpersonal inherent value are *grounded* in empirical knowledge when sufficient facts are adduced to allow the inference that probably a considerable number of the members of the group will find satisfaction in the object, or would find such satisfaction under the proper conditions. The relevant facts here are usually that the object in question has certain characteristics in common with other objects that have been experienced as possessing inherent value in the past, or the object in question has been found valuable by competent members of the group. One task of the art critic, of course, is to discover the characteristics shared by good works of art, and then to detect their presence or absence in any newly presented work.

The *felt normative force* of judgments of interpersonal inherent value derives largely from the attraction of the predicted satisfactions and the recognized competence of the speaker. Dependent upon the nature of the group and the extent of the individuals' identification with it, the belief that the object in question is or will be found valuable by other members of the group may add considerably to the normative force of the judgment.

As with judgments of personal inherent value, the justification or *warrant* of these interpersonal value ascriptions requires not only a verification of the facts presented as a ground and establishment of the validity of the inference from them, but also the justification of a judgment of interpersonal contributory value—a judgment to the effect that the satisfactions to be found are worth having *for the group or community.* When this has been done we have a fully warranted judgment. The problems of justifying judgments of interpersonal contributory value will be discussed below.

Judgments of interpersonal *instrumental* value are *grounded* when sufficient facts are presented to allow the inference that the object or action judged will be instrumental to satisfactions for members of the group in general, or, if the group is a community or being considered as a community, will be instrumental to achieving acknowledged community goals, or is in accord with a relevant regulative principle generally accepted by the community.

The normative force of judgments of interpersonal instrumental value may be related to all of the sources previously mentioned—the attraction of the goal, the compulsion of the situation, the force of the language itself, the authority of the speaker. In addition, when the judgment ascribes value relative to a community, a powerful source of authority lies in the identification of the individual with the community. As a member of the community he shares community interests, and community goals have a normative appeal for him, even though they would not otherwise directly provide satisfactions for him.

Similarly, as a member of the community, he ordinarily accepts the regulative principles generally accepted in the community and feels them as authoritative for his actions. These principles are, no matter who actually utters them, spoken with the voice of the community, a voice of which the individual's is a part, and as such they are charged with authority for him—an authority usually not felt to be completely externally imposed. Even when particular regulative principles seem unacceptable to the individual, they are felt as authoritative because they *are* accepted by the community of which he is a member. Hence he does not feel free to reject them simply because they interfere with his personal satisfactions, but rather feels it necessary to speak with the voice of the community in rejecting them.

If a regulative principle is accepted by the community, then the mere fact that adherence to the principle inconveniences an individual in some particular instance is not felt to be a sufficient reason for rejecting the principle. If the principle is to be rejected, it must be on some such ground as that it does not in fact further the achievement of community goals and thus would be rejected *by the community* if this were understood. For example, the individual may argue as a member of a subgroup in the community that adherence to this particular principle inflicts injury on this subgroup and so injures the community as a whole more than would rejection of the principle; or he may contend that the particular principle has been uncritically carried over from the past and has been rendered invalid by changing conditions, that it no longer operates to further community welfare. Or, if the principle in question does work to further acknowledged community ends, the individual who wishes to reject it must do so in the name of a wider community that contains the present community as a part, and argue that the principle is at variance with the goals of this wider community and thus, in the long view, is injurious to the present community as well. Mead has written:

> The only way in which we can react against the disapproval of the entire community is by setting up a higher sort of community which in a certain sense outvotes the one we find. A person may reach a point of going against the whole world about him; he may stand out by himself over against it. But to do so he has to speak with the voice of reason to himself. He has to comprehend the voices of the past and of the future. That is the only way the self can get a voice which is more than the voice of the community.[23]

The authority that the principles of a community hold for its individual members stems not only from the individual's present identification with the community, but also from his need to *continue* as a member. One cannot remain a member of a community while rejecting *all* of its principles. The number that may be rejected without loss of membership varies with communities, but in every community some basic principles *must* be accepted. Each refusal by an individual to accept a generally accepted principle threatens his membership in the community to some degree; hence, if the principle is to be rejected, it must be rejected by him *as a member of the community speaking for the community* and not merely as an individual, else he separates himself from the community.

The provision of a warrant for judgments of interpersonal instrumental value requires the justification of a judgment of interpersonal contributory value. A judgment of instrumental value is warranted, both its cognitive content and normative force justified, when the empirical statements upon which it is grounded are verified, the validity of the inferences assured, and the goal to which the object or action is instrumental is certified as a worthy goal, or the regulative principle with which the action accords is warranted.

The justification of any normative judgment of interpersonal value, as of any normative judgment of personal value, presupposes the warranting of a judgment of contributory value. If the value judgment *merely* predicts the attainment of some end or classifies some object as better or worse than other objects of its kind, it is only *indirectly* normative and we are mistaken in taking it to imply that the object ought₀ to be desired. The implication that it ought₀ to be desired is warranted only when it has been established that the satisfactions that the object provides or to which the object is instrumental are worth having.

When judgments of interpersonal value refer to a group that is *not* a community, the only sort of justification possible is to establish the probability that the ends being evaluated will contribute more to the goodness of life of all of the individuals forming the group than will the alternatives. Except for very small groups we cannot, in general, do this by considering each individual in turn, but must be able to establish the probability for the group by some other method. In many instances we can do this, since the ends involved are often the creation of conditions that make a good life possible, or satisfactions of a sort long experience has shown to be contributory to a good life for humans in general under normal conditions, for example, such ends as health, better working conditions, a higher standard of living, opportunity for education and recreation.

These goals are so generally acknowledged as worthy goals that usually when we make judgments of instrumental value for a group the worthiness of the end is assumed as proven, so the only further justification required for the judgment is that it be grounded in empirical knowledge. However, this is itself by no means always a simple matter; great uncertainties and well-nigh irreconcilable disagreements may arise as to what means will achieve some end, or which among alternative means will achieve it at least cost. Any accurate survey of the human scene, past or present, will reveal, I believe, that by far the majority of issues over which individuals and groups bitterly and often violently disagree are those concerning the means to commonly acknowledged general ends. In our present state of knowledge it is highly gratuitous to assume that all value problems are solved once agreement has been reached on general goals.

When a judgment of interpersonal contributory value refers to a community, the problem of justification is further complicated. Here it is not sufficient as justification to show that the ends in question contribute in general to the good life of the present individual members of the community. It must also be shown that the ends contribute to the good of the community as a community—they promote community goals, or at least do not interfere with them. The judgment may be warranted even if the end in question is not directly contributory to the good of the present individual members, if it can be shown to be necessary for the survival and stability of the community,[24] and hence indirectly contributory to the good of the individual members.

This is not to say that the goals of stability and survival of the community are ultimate and justify any means of attaining them. These goals, like any other community goal, must be subject to examination and evaluation, and in some circumstances may not prove to be worthy. Any community goal can be justified only by being shown to contribute to the goodness of the lives of the members of the community—future as well as present members, since the community is always conceived as growing, continuing, persisting through changes in the identity of its membership. If a community has become such that its survival as a community would not contribute to the welfare of its members, then its survival is not a warranted goal. In such circumstances a reorganization of the community is called for, a redirection of its aims so as to bring them into harmony with the individual's good. If no other means of such reorganization can be effective, revolution may be justified.

The goodness of an individual's life is dependent upon his being a member of some community. Human life apart from any community would be, in Hobbes's terms, "solitary, poore, nasty, brutish and short." But this does not mean that any community whatever ought, to be maintained, or even any community is better than no community; we may envision communities in which life is not only nasty, brutish, and short, but also filled with terrors far worse than those to be encountered in the wilderness. The resolution of the situation is not to have no community, but to have a better community. A better community is one in which the individual members lead a better life. A good community is one in which the good life of the individual members is not achieved in spite of the restrictions placed on him by the community, but rather because of and with aid of these restrictions. I am not saying that happiness and freedom consist in obedience to the law; rather, good laws are those instrumental to the happiness and freedom of the community.

Many of the most cherished goals of a community are not such as to provide direct satisfaction for its members but, again, to create and maintain the conditions under which satisfactions may be had. Political and religious freedom, legal equality, security from aggression, edu-

---

[24] Here "necessary" means either the only method of maintaining stability or surviving, or the method most efficient while least restrictive to the members of the community.

cational and economic opportunity are such goals. Any of these goals may be warranted by establishing that the lives of the members of the community will in general be better under these conditions and the maintenance of these conditions does not threaten the survival of the community. If it is found that adherence to some such goal does threaten community survival, then the task becomes one of determining the minimum degree in which the goal can be changed while removing the threat to the community. For, though abandonment of the goal altogether may be much better than destruction of the community, it may be much worse than survival of the community with continued adherence to a slightly altered goal. It may also be that abandonment, or restriction, of a particular goal itself offers a greater threat to the survival of the community than does continued adherence to the goal.

The establishment of any of these goals as warranted is not ever an easy task, usually requiring more knowledge than any of us have at the time decisions must be made. But this unavoidable fact does not support the contention that all value judgments are merely expressions of emotion or of volitional decisions, or that the only connection of beliefs to value judgments is a causal one. We can in any problem only seek to acquire as much knowledge as we can and use what knowledge we have. And when we conclude from this partial knowledge that something is good, or ought$_e$ to be done, this conclusion need no more be purely emotive or volitional than a scientific statement similarly based on partial knowledge.

The regulative principles accepted by a community and felt as binding by members of the community must be warranted in the only manner in which any regulative statement can be warranted—by being shown to be instrumental to a warranted goal. Hence, the justification of those judgments of instrumental value that are grounded by being shown to be in accord with an accepted regulative principle requires an additional step. It must be shown that adherence to the principle is a necessary condition of achieving the goal (or at least, that it will be instrumental to achieving the goal and not more restrictive than alternative means), and that the goal is a warranted goal.

In this chapter I have been concerned only with judgments of evaluation—statements about what is, was, will be, or would be better for some person, group, or community. Some of the judgments discussed might also be judgments of obligation; I have not here considered that possibility, but wish to repeat that nothing I have said is intended to deny it. In this chapter my concern with these statements has been only as judgments of evaluation. If they have an obligatory aspect, it presents a problem for the subsequent chapters, not this one.

In this chapter I have also avoided any but the briefest reference to the problems presented by conflicts of value. These problems must be faced by any theory that hopes to be at all complete; but I prefer to put off discussion of them until after the analysis of judgments of obligation. One point, however, may be noted here: even though there should prove to be no empirical method of deciding between conflicting value statements asserting some action to be good or bad with reference to different communities, the empirical status of the original judgments of evaluation is in no way changed. It may be quite true that a particular state of affairs may be good for community A and bad for community B, even if we cannot say what would be good for A-and-B.

A few general remarks may be in order in conclusion. All judgments of evaluation must refer to the welfare of some specific group. Those professing to assert what is good in general must be interpreted as referring to the group of all humans, the ideal community of man. But even those judgments which refer to smaller groups need not be less objective for being thus relative. We would, however, often avoid confusion if the range of the group were specified.

All, or almost all, judgments of evaluation are judgments about what is *better* or *worse*, rather than about what is categorically good or bad. The values we find in immediate experience, the satisfactions and dissatisfactions encountered in living, may be experienced as absolute goods or absolute evils, but whenever we make a *judgment* of evaluation, we judge one state of affairs to be better or worse than some other, some action more likely to contribute to the goodness of life than would others. It is only because these judgments are comparative that we are enabled to make them empirically; if the judgment could not be arrived at by a comparison of alternatives, we would have no means of arriving at it without recourse to dogma or some undiscovered process of intuition.

Another result of our analysis is this: a major share of the felt normative force of judgments of evaluation derives from the attraction and appeal of the goal judged to be good. Hence we often do not feel motivated by the judgment unless we *believe* the goal to be good as asserted; that is, unless we believe attainment of the goal will contribute to a good life for us or for the community. Thus, far from its being the case that statements cannot possibly be both normative and true, the functioning of judgments of evaluation as normative depends, in many instances, upon their being accepted as true; or, if you please, they are only felt to be normative because they are accepted as descriptive.

In no place in this chapter have I intended to suggest or imply that any of the objects or actions found to be warranted goods are *obligatory* for any persons. I have been concerned here only with what ought₀ to be, not with what ought₀ to be done. Merely on the basis of the preceding analysis we are not yet in a position to say, in most instances, what *finally* ought to be done; questions of obligation may be involved as well as questions of evaluation. The question of whether the goodness of any action or object itself imposes an obligation on any person is one that must be left to the next chapter.

Chapter V

JUDGMENTS OF OBLIGATION

EMPIRICISTS AND naturalistic philosophers have written neither as clearly nor as cogently about obligation as they have about evaluation. They have been, on the whole, either unwilling or unable to break away from ideas of obligation developed in the context of religious or metaphysical ethical theories, or when they have managed to dissociate themselves from such views, they have tended to the extreme of denying any validity at all to the notion of obligation. Consequently, though in empiricist writings lies a wealth of suggestions and indications of the form an adequate theory of obligation might take, I know of no such theory worked out in sufficient detail which I am willing to adopt as a basis for an analysis of judgments of obligation, as the Dewey-Lewis theory of valuation was adopted in the previous chapter.

It will be necessary, then, to find a theory of obligation that will be adequate without being nonempirical. In order to do this I shall consider briefly the religious and metaphysical tradition out of which contemporary theories of obligation have grown, and shall then examine some contemporary theories, showing the relation of most of these to this tradition and emphasizing the empiricist's failure to recognize the nature of the break with the traditional view his empiricism requires. I shall then propose a theory of obligation which I believe avoids most of the difficulties besetting these other theories.

The view of obligation prevalent throughout most of western history and civilization, at least, and still probably honored or explicitly avowed by a majority of western peoples, is one that finds obligations to result from the command of some supernatural authority.

In any religious community one of the primary functions of the deity, or those who speak for the deity, is to determine what is good and what is evil, what men ought to do and what they must not do. Those actions God commands, man has an obligation to perform; those ends God decrees good, man has an obligation to seek. In both the obligation arises not merely from the goodness of the end or action, but from the command of God. No matter what the decision in the medieval argument over whether God declared things to be good because He found them to be so, or they were good because He so declared them, man's way was clear; he was to seek the good because God decreed it, and what God decreed that he was to seek was thereby good. God's decrees are not only authoritative, they are indispensable; without them men would not *know* what is good nor have reason to avoid evil. The profundity of Voltaire's remark that if there were no God, it would be necessary to invent Him, is attested by the voices of the many who still echo Dostoievsky's cry, "If there is no God, then everything is permissible."

This view is not an unattractive one. Its great merit is that it allows men to know with certainty which acts are obligatory and which forbidden, what is good and what evil, without this knowledge resting on mere fallible human reason. It removes much of the difficulty of decision, much of the lingering doubt that may follow. Our obligations are clearly prescribed; all one needs is the strength of will to act on them. Those alternatives over which we should otherwise have to hesitate are not allowed the status of competing goods to be proven unworthy, but rather are looked upon as "temptations" to be overcome, which only our human frailty allows to appear attractive.

The philosophical counterpart of this religious tradition is the sort of metaphysical theory that finds goodness and obligation somehow embedded in the structure of the universe, perhaps in the nature of the Absolute, and discoverable to man through the use of Reason, which in later idealism itself becomes a manifestation of an underlying cosmic spirit realizing itself in history. This view shares with the religious one the attraction of certainty, but at a price. For the knowledge it allows is not a gift freely given by the deity to all, but must be reached by reason, a process in which not all men may succeed.

Aside from the certainty it offers, some characteristics of this traditional theory are worthy of note: (1) In both the religious and metaphysical versions, both value and obligation are independent of human thought and feeling. They continue to exist in the actual world whether or not we hear or heed the voice of God, whether or not we fathom the nature of the Absolute. They are neither constituted nor diminished by our knowing of them, our being or not being pleased or satisfied, feeling or not feeling compelled. We cannot rid ourselves of an obligation merely by deciding that we are no longer bound by it. And we may, in general, *correctly* assert that someone has an obligation without ourselves knowing anything about his present state of knowledge or his feelings or emotions. (2) In many instances we need not inquire into the consequences of an act to know it is obligatory—if it is an act of a certain kind, we have an obligation to perform it and no need to know more about it. (3) No real conflict can exist between value and obligation. We have an obligation to do what is good, imposed upon us either by God or the Absolute or written into the nature of the cosmos, and the goodness of those acts which are obligatory is likewise guaranteed by God or the nature of the universe. Apparent conflicts in particular cases are a result of our ignorance or our weakness in succumbing to temptation.

Most of these characteristics are preserved in the contemporary intuitionist theory, which, however, avoids the difficulties of having to prove the existence or intentions of God or plumb the depths of the Absolute. Obligation, for the intuitionist, is accounted for by the presence of a simple, unanalyzable, nonnatural quality of rightness, fittingness, or suitability directly intuited as a quality of occurrent situations or states of affairs. On this view obligation is an objective property of the situation, there whether we apprehend it or not, and in some instances knowable independently of any knowledge of consequences. But since there are, in some intuitionistic theories, several "right-making" characteristics, goodness being only one of them, it is possible to have conflicts between value and obligation. This difficulty is resolved, however, by the contention that we are able to intuit not only that actions are obligatory, but also degrees of rightness or suitability, and hence can "see" in the particular situation which actions are more incumbent on us.

It may be worth noting that these intuitionist theories adhere more closely to common sense than does any other contemporary theory. In fact, this strict adherence to common sense may be responsible for the weakness of the view. Be this as it may, in our common sense discussions of obligation, we do take obligations to exist independent of our thought or feeling and we do assert that some actions can be known to be obligatory without knowledge of the consequences. And where the intuitionist view departs from the religious tradition, it still remains close to common sense, for it is our experience that obligation and value conflict, that we have to choose between right and good on some occasions.

An intuitionist theory avoiding even this conflict between value and obligation is presented by G. E. Moore in *Principia Ethica*. Moore offers a nonnaturalistic analysis of "good" and then derives obligation from goodness, writing, ". . . to assert that a certain line of conduct is, at a given time, absolutely right or obligatory, is obviously to assert that more good or less evil will exist in the world, if it is adopted, than if anything else be done instead." (P. 25.) On this view the *one* source of obligation is the goodness to be produced by the act and hence no conflict between value and obligation is possible.

All these theories are perforce rejected by empiricists; neither the commands of God, the metaphysical structure of the cosmos, nor non-natural properties are open to empirical investigation. But in rejecting these theories, empiricists have not been clear about which of the accompanying characteristics their empirical theories might retain and which must be rejected as incompatible with empiricism, with the result that they have generally rejected some characteristics they might have retained and clung to the one most difficult to reconcile with their commitment to empiricism.

A survey of the theories of obligation defended by contemporary empiricists may give some substance to this contention.

The most radical of empiricist theories is, of course, that professed by the various noncognitive theorists. These philosophers do not see any necessity for distinguishing judgments of obligation from judgments of evaluation, since both, for them, are merely expressions of emotion or volition, without cognitive significance. The difference, if any, between the two sorts of judgment apparently lies in a difference in the sort of emotion expressed.

This theory, which its advocates claim to be the only one compatible with empiricism, denies any validity whatsoever to judgments of obligation and in doing so denies to obligation, of course, all the characteristics we found associated with the traditional and common sense views. Obligation obviously is not independent of human thought or feeling, since the only objective elements the noncognitive theory finds in judgments of obligation are the emotions or volitions expressed. The question of whether we may correctly say that someone has an obligation when he does not feel compelled is not to be taken seriously, since, on this view, we *never* can correctly say that anyone has an obligation. Similarly, the questions of whether an investigation of consequences is necessary for a justified attribution of obligation and whether there can be conflicts between value and obligation are not questions that admit of answers not themselves merely emotive or volitional.

This theory, which has proven so attractive to contemporary philosophers, is at odds not only with traditional views but also with our common sense ideas and our ordinary ways of speaking. But before we decide that common sense has been hopelessly infected by the traditional view and must be completely reëducated, or reconditioned, we may do well to inquire whether such radical measures are indeed necessary, as the noncognitivist claims.

Aside from noncognitivism, the theory of obligation most often espoused by naturalists is essentially the one defended by G. E. Moore, which in effect reduces obligation to evaluation, or, in more usual terms, rightness to goodness, though of course they reject Moore's nonnaturalistic analysis of "good." This has been the path traditionally taken by naturalistic philosophers and, despite the continued criticism of such theories, remains the path taken by many contemporaries. Today as in the past it is the view adopted by utilitarians.

Among many similar statements in the current literature, I may cite two as examples. Thus, one recent writer, after defining "good" in terms of satisfaction, states, "An individual's duty is to do that which is most deeply satisfactory to him in the long run.... I think that it is the absolutely true and the finally valid principle in ethics."[1]

Another contemporary utilitarian writes:

... a morally right action is simply any action such that probably no alternative open to the agent capable of voluntary action and of taking into account the evidence available to him, would be better (to the agent) and such that probably some alternative would be worse (to the agent).... the moral obligatoriness of actions is regarded as grounded in their probable instrumental value.[2]

We have noted three characteristics of the traditional view of obligation. In these naturalistic theories these characteristics are accorded the following treatment: the first is retained with some modification— if "good" is defined in terms of pleasure or satisfaction, then obligation cannot be completely independent of human feelings and still be derivative from goodness; yet we may still be able to say correctly that someone has an obligation without knowing anything about his present feelings, and it remains true that one cannot rid himself of an obligation merely by deciding he is not bound by it. The second is rejected— in these views we cannot know an act to be obligatory without having some knowledge of its probable consequences. The third is retained— clearly, if our only obligation is to do what is best, there can be no real conflict between value and obligation.

I wish to examine the relation of naturalism, or empiricism, to this third characteristic; it is my belief that, of the various aspects of the traditional view, this one is, in fact, incompatible with empiricism in ethics.

In traditional theories the obligation to do the good, and the guarantee of harmony between obligation and value, follow from the common supernatural source of both value and obligation. An important element in these views is that it is not merely the goodness of an action which renders it obligatory, but that it is commanded by God. The nat-

[1] G. Williams, "Normative Naturalistic Ethics," *The Journal of Philosophy*, XLVII (1950), 324.

[2] Ian McGreal, "A Naturalistic Utilitarianism," *ibid.*, pp. 523–524.

uralist philosophers quoted above also assume an obligation to do the good, but without the voice of God to provide authority and without, as far as I can tell, citing any substitute for God in this function.

All of these naturalistic theorists, along with G. E. Moore, seem to assume that the only obligatory acts are those that produce the greatest good, or, in other terms, the *only* obligation we have is to produce the greatest good. If nothing else, this formulation seems a bit strong since many people have thought we have obligations other than this one; consequently, I wish to consider at length a weaker statement implied by it: (Actions productive of maximum good are obligatory, merely because they are productive of maximum good) A similar statement has been made by Sir W. D. Ross, "... it seems self-evident that if there are things that are intrinsically good, it is *prima facie* a duty to bring them into existence rather than not to do so, and to bring as much of them into existence as possible."[3] The question here, that is, is not whether goodness is the *only* ground of obligation, but whether it is, by itself, a ground of obligation at all. I do not intend to deny that we ever have obligations to perform acts productive of good, but only to deny that this obligation stems merely from the goodness to be produced.

If the statement "actions productive of maximum good are obligatory, merely because they are productive of maximum good" is to be true, it must be either an empirical statement, a synthetic a priori statement, or a tautology. G. E. Moore calls it "obvious"; Ross, "self-evident." It is not clear from these statements whether Ross and Moore claim to intuit a necessary connection between goodness and obligation, intending their statements as synthetic a priori, or what. But this is not a major difficulty for them, since the synthetic a priori holds no terrors for the intuitionists. This alternative cannot be accepted by empiricists, however; neither can they be content merely to call the statement "self-evident" or "obvious." Let us, then, inquire into what status it may have in an empiricist theory.

Consider first the possibility that the statement is (empirical.) If it were, it would not then be an analysis of obligation, but would presuppose some such analysis, which these naturalists have not yet given. If the statement that actions productive of maximum good are therefore obligatory is empirical, then we must have some method of determining that an act is obligatory, independent of our determining that

[3] "What Makes Right Acts Right," in Sellars and Hospers, eds., *Readings in Ethical Theory* (New York: Appleton-Century-Crofts, 1952), p. 181; reprinted from *The Right and the Good*.

it is productive of maximum good. But naturalists have not provided any such method; rather the only method they propose for determining that an act is obligatory is that of determining that it is productive of maximum good. Hence, they cannot intend the statement as empirical but as analytic—presumably feeling that it follows from the meaning of "good" that good acts are obligatory.

So, let us turn to the alternative that the statement is tautological, that it follows from the meaning of "good" that acts productive of maximum good are obligatory. This would seem to be a tenable assertion for the defenders of a religious or metaphysical theory, who define "good" in terms of God's declarations or the ultimate nature of the Absolute, but is it equally tenable for empiricists?

The naturalists we have quoted all define "good" in terms of satisfaction, pleasure, interest or desire, as have most philosophers who choose to accept as good that which is found to be good in experience. Now, we must ask, is there anything about satisfactions, pleasures, interests, or desires that makes actions producing or realizing them obligatory? Can it be said that one has an obligation to seek satisfactions or pleasures, to pursue his interests or fulfill his desires merely because they are satisfactions, interests, etc.? We need only ask this to see that it is not so in any sense of "obligation" we ordinarily use in moral discourse.

If this is not already clear, let us consider some examples. If the tendency of an action to produce more satisfactions or more fully realize interests than any other in itself makes the act obligatory, then *any* act producing more satisfactions, etc., must be obligatory. Suppose a man who has been cast adrift on a raft and has not eaten for several days lands on an island and discovers food. Eating will surely be the most satisfying action he can perform, and we may assume it will be the act that in the circumstances will most fully realize his interests. But we should never say that he has an *obligation* to eat *merely because eating would satisfy him*. We might, indeed, say he ought to eat, but this is an "ought$_e$," and cannot be translated into "has an obligation."

Or suppose a young man is deliberating over what to do on a Saturday evening. The alternatives he contemplates are: going to a movie with Gloria, going to a dance with Mary, staying at home and reading a novel, visiting a sick friend. And suppose he concludes correctly that the greatest satisfaction is to be had in dancing with Mary. Are we to say then that he has an obligation to ask Mary for a date?

It may be interposed that by including the alternative of visiting the sick friend I have prejudiced the issue, since this introduces a conflicting obligation. But we never in fact consider such a situation to be one of conflicting obligations; rather, we view it as a conflict between obligation and interest, which supports the point that we do not ordinarily think of satisfaction or interest as imposing any obligation on us. We may exclude the alternative of visiting the sick friend and reconsider the example. No matter what course the young man decides he ought. to pursue, we should call none of them obligatory. The situation, as described, is just not one in which obligation is involved, *even though satisfaction and interest are involved.*

Even if in this example our young man considers not only his own satisfactions and interests, but also those of the other persons affected, we would still not ordinarily say that any of the alternatives are obligatory. Suppose the young man—yet us call him Joe—believes correctly that if he doesn't ask Mary to the dance, another young man, John, will and Mary will find more satisfaction in going with John than with Joe. And Joe further believes correctly that the satisfactions he and Gloria will derive from each staying at home with a novel are greater than the satisfaction they would derive from going to the movie together. Is our conclusion, then, that Joe has an *obligation* to stay at home with his novel? The very suggestion is ludicrous.

The conclusion is that if "good" is naturalistically defined, then we do not have an obligation to perform acts productive of maximum good, merely because they are productive of maximum good, and a fortiori this is not our only obligation.

The point I wish to make is that *once goodness has been defined in terms of satisfaction, pleasure, interest, or desire,* it does not follow from the meaning of "good" that acts productive of good are obligatory, if we wish to retain at all the common sense meaning of "obligation." The critics of naturalism have belabored this point, though not in just these terms, but the force of the criticism seems not to have been felt by naturalists.

The naturalists have taken over from the traditional religious view the idea that we have an obligation to perform good actions, but they deny the religious definition of "good" that makes it plausible. And they have not been sufficiently aware that in the tradition it was not merely that an act was productive of good which made it obligatory, but that it was productive of *God-decreed* goodness. It is only when goodness is defined in such religious or metaphysical terms that it becomes tautologous that men have an obligation to perform good acts.

When "good" has been defined in terms of pleasure, interest, satisfaction, or desire, the critics have asked, "But why ought. I maximize my satisfactions?" or "Why ought$_o$ men most fully realize their interests?"; and they have interpreted the failure of naturalists to give a satisfactory answer as an indication of the refutation of naturalism. For, given his empiricist definition of "good," the naturalist faced with these questions has no satisfactory answer beginning "You have an obligation because...." But he does, nevertheless, have a satisfactory answer. This answer is: "You have no such obligation! It is tautologous that you ought$_e$ do what is productive of the most good, but that you ought$_o$ do so is an empirical statement whose truth or falsity cannot be ascertained apart from a consideration of the particular context."

Once the empiricist gives up as impossible his attempt to show a necessary connection between "good" and "obligation" or "duty" and "interest," he may face the problem of obligation free from the assumption that has heretofore made an adequate analysis unattainable. It is for this reason that I have gone to such lengths to stress the need for empirical philosophers to distinguish between judgments of evaluation and judgments of obligation.

We have not yet considered one naturalistic view of obligation that may seem to avoid some of the difficulties mentioned—the pragmatist theory which bases obligation on "the requirements of the situation." The contention is that, given a problematic situation involving a person or persons, there are objective requirements in the situation. In view of these requirements, the situation "makes a claim" on the agent. Obligations are then correlated with these claims.

This theory sounds more plausible than the others we have discussed, but even so cannot be accepted as it stands. The assertion that there are objective requirements in the situation must mean the facts of the situation are such that some particular actions will probably lead to a satisfactory resolution of the problem while others will not. Those leading to a satisfactory resolution are then said to be required by the situation. In virtue of these requirements the situation makes a claim on the agent, who then has an obligation. But if we follow this up, this view encounters the same difficulties as those already discussed. The same examples apply to it and with the same effect. We should again have to assert that the hungry man has an obligation to eat, and Joe has an obligation to ask Mary to the dance or to stay at home with his novel. And these assertions are all repugnant to common sense and ordinary usage.

What makes the view seem more plausible than the others is that it correlates obligations with *claims,* and this agrees with our experience of obligation. But what makes it unacceptable is the notion of claims "made by the situation." For situations cannot literally make claims; it is only persons or groups of persons who can make claims. To say that a situation makes a claim is to use "makes a claim" metaphorically, and since this is only a metaphorical claim, it can only be correlated with a metaphorical obligation. Not metaphorical but literal obligations interest us here.

Hence we must reject this theory along with the others. But we may salvage from it the key notion that obligations are to be correlated with claims.

The idea that obligations arise from the making of a claim was put forth by William James, who saw also that claims must be made by persons, not by situations. James wrote:

> But the moment we take a steady look at the question, *we see not only that without a claim actually made by some concrete person there can be no obligation, but that there is some obligation wherever there is a claim.* Claim and obligation are, in fact, coextensive terms; they cover each other exactly....
> ... every de facto claim creates in so far forth [*sic*] an obligation. We inveterately think that something which we call the 'validity' of the claim is what gives it its obligatory character, and that this validity is something outside of the claims mere existence as a matter of fact.... But again, how can such an inorganic abstract character of imperativeness, additional to the imperativeness which is concrete in the claim itself, *exist?* Take any demand, however slight, which any creature, however weak, may make. Ought it not, for its own sake, be satisfied? If not prove why not. The only possible kind of proof you could adduce would be the exhibition of another creature who should make a demand which ran the other way. The only possible reason there can be why any phenomenon ought to exist is that such a phenomenon actually is desired. Any desire is imperative to the extent of its amount; it makes itself valid by the fact that it exists at all.[4]

In this passage James seems to use "claim" as equivalent to "demand," but we usually take a claim to be something more than this; we take it to be a demand purported to be valid—a demand asserted as rightful. But either way, if we are to heed common sense and ordinary usage, we must disagree with James's assertion that *every* claim creates some obligation to satisfy it. We surely do *not* believe that *any* claim or demand *any* person may make creates an obligation to satisfy it. Suppose a stranger whom I meet in the street demands that I give him my life savings, or an indolent, failing student demands that he be given an A in each of his courses, or an illiterate dimwit claims he ought to be appointed president of Harvard. Do we in any sense think that the claimee, the person against whom the claim or demand is made, has *any* obligation to satisfy the demands? I think not. We

---

[4] *The Will to Believe* (London: Longmans, Green and Company, 1899), pp. 194–195.

should brush the claims aside on the ground that they have no validity.

Despite James's protest we have to conclude that obligations are not to be correlated with every claim, but only with every valid claim. What misleads James is the ambiguity of "ought." When he asks, "Ought it not, for its own sake, be satisfied?" and assumes an affirmative answer, he thinks this then shows the existence of some obligation. But this is not so; and it is only made to seem so by James's failure to distinguish "ought$_e$" from "ought$_o$." If we take the "ought" in his question to be "ought$_e$," then an affirmative answer may seem reasonable; the question is then "Would it not be better if it were, for its own sake, satisfied?" But even if true this confers no obligation. If we take the "ought" as "ought$_o$."—"Does not someone have an obligation to satisfy it, for its own sake?"—the answer must be "No."

The positive result of this survey of empiricist theories of obligation is that obligations arise from and are to be correlated with valid claims. We may take this as a starting point for analysis. Obligation is a relationship involving persons and acts. Only persons can either make or be the object of valid claims. We may correctly assert a statement of the form "A has an obligation to perform act X" only when some person exists who has made a valid claim (or for whom a valid claim has been made), a claim that would be satisfied by A's performance of act X.

In order to have a complete analysis of obligation it is necessary to provide an explication of the notion of a *valid claim,* since obligations exist only when there are valid claims. I propose to investigate the concept of a valid claim by considering some clear-cut instances of obligation, instances in which we should agree without hesitation that someone has an obligation to perform some particular action.

I shall compare three examples: (a) Bob and Joe agree one spring day that Joe will spade Bob's garden on Saturday and Bob will mow Joe's lawn on Sunday. On Saturday Joe works diligently in Bob's garden while Bob lolls on the beach. On Sunday Bob awakens, looks out on a bright fair day, and thinks this too would be a fine day to spend at the beach. But while he is preparing, Joe, who knows Bob's habits, calls to remind him, "You know, you have to mow my lawn today."

In this situation we are able to say that Bob does have an obligation without our knowing any more about his thoughts or feelings. Further, he cannot rid himself of the obligation merely by deciding that he is not bound by it. And we are able to assert that Bob has this obligation without having to consider the consequences of his action. Also, if Bob correctly believes that the most satisfactory action would be to go to the beach, there will be a conflict between value and obligation.

Now consider two other examples, which are significant in their differences. (*b*) An acquaintance of mine tells me that he would be delighted if I would come to a dinner he is planning. Not being sure of the state of my affairs, or my attitudes, I reply, "Well, perhaps; I'll see if I can make it."

Later another friend asks me to go with him to the ball game on the night of the proposed dinner, and I accept, thinking that I shall enjoy the ball game more than the dinner and feeling free to accept because I have no obligation to go to the dinner. When the acquaintance calls and says, "I'm counting on you for dinner, you know," I can simply tell him, "Sorry, I can't make it. Perhaps some other time." No other explanation is necessary, since I had no obligation.

(*c*) An acquaintance tells me he would be delighted if I would come to a dinner he is planning. I reply, "Of course. I will surely come."

Later when a friend asks me to go to the ball game, I regretfully decline because I have an obligation to attend the dinner. If some unforeseen occurrence makes it impossible for me to attend, I feel it necessary to call and make some explanation other than merely, "Sorry, I can't come." Some circumstances may nullify my obligation to attend the dinner—if I am ill or called out of town, for example—but even though these occurrences excuse me from performance of the obligatory act, I then have an obligation to explain my failure to perform it.

In all three of these examples a claim is made upon a person by another person. But while the claimee clearly has an obligation to satisfy the claim in two of the instances, he equally clearly does not in the other. In (*a*) and (*c*) the claim is valid; in (*b*) it is not. What makes the claim valid in one instance and not in another is the making of a *commitment,* the performance of some act by the claimee which binds him to honor the claim.

Obligations arise from claims validated by commitments. If obligation is construed in this manner, it is understandable that we are often able to assert that someone has an obligation without having to inquire into the consequences of the act. For, in these simple situations, to verify that someone has an obligation we need only verify that a previous act of commitment has occurred. Thus, at least in some instances, a statement of the form "*A* has an obligation to do *X*" is as open to empirical verification as is, say, the statement "Jones is a landowner." In neither can we verify the statement merely by observing the subsequent actions of the person mentioned, but we can do so by verifying that some action occurred in the past.

We are thus led to the notion of *commitment* as central in the analysis of obligation. It is my belief that the analysis can be completely carried through in these terms; it can be truly asserted that someone has an obligation only when there has been some form of commitment which validates a claim.[5]

The crucial question is, of course, whether this analysis will cover the whole range of circumstances in which we ordinarily want to say someone has an obligation, or if not, which have to be excluded. It is of course possible to arbitrarily limit "obligation" to apply only to instances that satisfy the requirements of the analysis, but if by doing so we have to leave out a great many of what are usually considered obligations, we must take care to ensure that not our analysis but ordinary usage is at fault. The point immediately at issue is whether the concept of *commitment* is broad enough to correlate with all generally admitted instances of obligation.

There are three general forms of commitment. I shall discuss these separately in some detail.

(1) *Explicit commitments,* such as those occurring in the examples discussed previously, are the most easily identified and verified commitments, and most readily acknowledged.

In every language and culture there are a number of particular linguistic and behavioral forms appropriate to and commonly used for the specific purpose of making a commitment, of binding oneself to something, of placing oneself under obligation. What David Hume said of *promises,* "... there is a certain form of words ... by which we bind ourselves to the performance of any action," is equally true of an indefinite number of forms in every culture. We may bind ourselves to the performance of an action by use of the phrases: I promise to ..., I agree to ..., I will ..., I swear to ..., I vow to ..., I guarantee to ..., I resolve to ..., You have my assurance that ..., I give you my word, and many more. We may likewise bind ourselves by any one of a number of nonlinguistic forms—a handshake, a significant nod, a raising of

---

[5] I am here, as throughout this chapter, primarily concerned with *moral* obligation and not with legal obligation. Many of our legal obligations also arise from commitments, for example, the signing of a contract, but the act of making a commitment is not, in general, a necessary condition for legal obligation. We may have a legal obligation to obey the laws of any nation or territory we happen to be in, for example, no matter what the circumstances of our arrival there and no matter what commitments we may have made. And we may of course have a moral obligation to refuse to comply with some legal obligation, but this does not ordinarily cancel or annul the legal obligation.

the hand in the manner of taking an oath. Or we may bind ourselves by signing our name to a contract or agreement. In performing any of these actions we place ourselves under obligation. Barring extenuating circumstances to be discussed later, the fact that we have an obligation may be established merely by verifying that we have performed the act of commitment and that the claim thereby validated is made.

We not only make such explicit commitments for ourselves, in some matters other persons may make explicit commitments for us. Thus parents may make commitments for their children, a wife for her husband, an agent or lawyer for his client, etc., and such commitments are considered binding. The question of whether one person may commit another, and the extent of the commitments he may make, depends upon the particular relationship existing between the two.

(2) *Implicit commitments* include the commitments entailed by the explicit commitments we may make, and the commitments implied in the claims we make on others.

Most explicit commitments carry with them further commitments that are understood by all of the persons involved, though not actually stated. Thus, in some instances, if I commit myself to bring about a certain state of affairs, it is implied that I will do so by the best means at my disposal. Or if I commit myself to perform some action, certain implied conditions may be understood. If I borrow a book and agree to return it in a week, I also commit myself to return it in the same condition as when borrowed. So, even if I return the book as agreed, should there be several pages missing, it would be felt I still have not fulfilled my obligation. Further, it is almost always understood that if intervening circumstances prevent my fulfilling an explicit obligation, I am obliged to explain my failure and, if possible, to make suitable compensation.

A familiar sort of implicit commitment is made by accepting a position or office, or becoming a part of some organization. Whether we sign a contract, take an oath of office, or merely have our name added to a payroll, in accepting a role in the organization we commit ourselves to accept as authoritative the directives of our superiors in the organization, to perform honestly the function of our particular role or station, to refrain from actions injurious to the organization.

In general the specific nature of the entailed commitment depends upon the nature and conditions of the explicit commitment.

A second and perhaps more important sort of implicit commitment is implied in the claims one person may make upon others when explicit commitments have not been made. When I make such a claim upon someone else, I, in effect, assert that claims of this sort are valid within the community in which I make the claim and in so doing commit myself to honor such claims when they are made on me by a member of the community. Thus when I assert my right to some property, when I call something "mine," I am asserting and recognizing the validity of claims of ownership within the community; I commit myself to honor rightful claims to property. In short, I acknowledge my obligation not to steal. Similarly, when I demand truthfulness in others, I commit myself to speak truly; when I denounce political apathy, I commit myself to take an active interest in political affairs, etc.[6]

We are, perhaps understandably, often less willing to admit our implicit commitments than our explicit ones, but we are usually quick to recognize the implicit commitments of others. Implicit commitments and the obligations correlated with them are often more difficult to verify than are explicit ones. Not being anywhere spelled out in detail, their specific content is less easily discernible; in many instances no criterion may be at hand to enable us to decide between conflicting opinions about whether or not someone has an obligation. This must not, however, lead us to assert that, therefore, no ascriptions of obligation are verifiable, or even that no ascriptions of obligations arising from implicit commitments are verifiable, for often the content of the implied commitment is clear and the commitment is clearly made.

(3) The third form of commitment is one we make, or are held to have made, merely by our continuing *membership in a community*.

In the previous chapter the notion of a community and the status of the individual as a member of communities emerged as a crucial factor in our analysis of judgments of evaluation. The existence of the community and the individual in the community is at least as important for any analysis of obligation. In each of the various communities of which an individual is a member, his very acceptance of a particular role in the community, as indicated by his continuing to function in that role, commits him in various ways to the individuals in the community and to the community as a whole. As a husband, a wife, a parent, a child, a student, a teacher, a club member, a citizen of city, state or nation, a friend, a neighbor, a Democrat, a union member, a church member, he is not merely an individual but an individual with a certain status in a living community. And this status carries with it responsibilities and rights; by being a member of the community we

---

[6] Cf. John Dewey and James Tufts, *Ethics*, rev. ed., (New York: Henry Holt & Company, 1932), p. 251.

acknowledge the responsibilities, commit ourselves to them, and also assert our claim to the rights. As Arthur Murphy writes:

When and in so far as men are members of a moral community and act as its members, they have a right to share in the goods of that community. Except as actual or potential sharers in its goods and responsibilities, they have and can have no "rights" at all, and there is no sense, though among the gullible there may be some advantage, in claiming them.[7]

As Murphy recognizes, membership in the community carries with it rights and responsibilities. The "rights" one has are correlated with commitments and obligations. Any enjoyment of some right in the community commits one to some share in the responsibilities of the community. For one member of a community to enjoy a right requires that other members assume some obligation, and the member enjoying the right thereby also is committed to assume similar obligations toward other members of the community.

Commitments are implied in our continuing to function as a member of the community and, whether we explicitly acknowledge them or not, we are held to them by the rest of the community unless we explicitly disavow them—and this is not always permissible. There are some commitments which we must acknowledge in order to remain a member of the community; adherence to them is a condition of our continued membership. If we disavow them we terminate our membership. And where, as in a national political community, we cannot become physically separated from the community, we may be regarded as outlaws—proscribed from enjoying any rights in the community, yet still subject to punishment.

Sometimes these commitments are made explicit—we take a marriage vow, become a naturalized citizen, pledge allegiance to a nation, are initiated into a club, fraternity or association, swear to uphold some office to which we are appointed or elected. But more often our membership in a community is not so formally inaugurated; we are born into a family, city, state, and nation; we automatically assume the rights and duties of citizenship. But that these commitments are not formally undertaken makes them no less real.

The commitments attending our membership in a community are many and varied. In any community, membership commits us to abide by the rules of the community, to obey its laws. Once one is aware of

[7] *The Uses of Reason* (New York: Macmillan, 1943), p. 168. Cf. *also* G. H. Mead, *Mind, Self and Society* (Chicago: University of Chicago Press, 1934), pp. 203 and 381.

these rules and continues to act as a member of the community, he is held to be committed to be bound by these rules. The classic presentation of this point is still that made by Socrates, as presented by Plato:

> Then the laws will say, "Consider, Socrates, if we are speaking truly that in your present attempt you are going to do us an injury. For, having brought you into the world, and nurtured and educated you, and given you and every other citizen a share in every good which we had to give, we further proclaim to any Athenian by the liberty which we allow him, that if he does not like us when he has become of age and has seen the ways of the city, and made our acquaintance, he may go where he pleases and take his goods with him. None of us laws will forbid him or interfere with him.... But he who has experience of the manner in which we order justice and administer the state, and still remains, has entered into an implied contract that he will do as we command him. And he who disobeys us is, as we maintain, thrice wrong ... thirdly because he has made an agreement with us that he will duly obey our commands; and he neither obeys them nor convinces us that our commands are unjust; and we do not rudely impose them, but give him the alternative of obeying or convincing us—that we offer, and he does neither.[8]

As we are committed to obey the laws, so we are committed to honor the moral standards of the community, to accept as regulative the principles accepted by the community—to accept them or convince the community that they are wrong. We are *not* committed to unquestioning obedience of either the laws or the moral standards of the community; but we are committed to accept them as binding until we can show them to be unjustified; and even then, as long as we remain a member of the community, to accept them as binding until we have persuaded the community that they are unjustified.[9]

It is in our commitments to the community that the obligation to perform actions productive of good arises. As a member of the community we are held by the community to be committed to the adoption of community goals and the furtherance of the common *good*. This is a condition of our acceptance and our continuance as a member of the community. Hence we become obligated to perform acts productive of this common good; but the obligation does *not* arise merely from the goodness to be produced, rather it arises from the fact that it is a goodness *for a community of which we are a member and to which we are committed*. It is our commitment to the goals of the community through our participation in the community and our sharing of its benefits which renders the action obligatory.

We are often more willing to acknowledge the commitments entailed in our participation in a community than we are the implied commit-

---

[8] *Crito*, tr. by B. Jowett, 51.

[9] I shall consider later the problem of conflicting obligations, obviously pertinent at this point.

ments discussed above. This is largely owing to our identification with the community, our dependence upon the community for the realization of our own values, the degree of the involvement of the self in the life of the community. We acknowledge the commitments because, as we are a part of the community, it is a part of us. And further, refusal to acknowledge them threatens our continued membership in the community.

I am aware of the vagueness of the idea of a community and of membership in a community. And I am surely not prepared to draw in detail the outlines or limits of community, or describe with any precision the essential nature of communities. This is work yet to be done. Nor can I specify necessary and sufficient conditions for membership in a community. Physical presence within the confines of a community is surely not sufficient to constitute membership. Rather, the individual must *function* as a member, consider himself a member and be so considered by the remainder of the community. The task of exploring this in detail is also work yet to be done.

The vagueness of the concepts of community and membership in a community makes it difficult in many instances to determine just what obligations a given individual may have or verify a statement ascribing an obligation. But, I must insist again, this difficulty must not lead us to assert that ascriptions of obligation are in general or in principle unverifiable; in a great many situations we can determine quite precisely what a person's commitments are.

There is an overlapping of the three types of commitments which sometimes simplifies the problem of verifying ascriptions of obligation. The commitments implied by our membership in a community are often also implied in the claims we make on others, and commitments of both these types are often made explicit.

In this discussion of commitment and obligation I have made no mention of either "commitment to oneself" or "obligation to oneself." I do not consider these central in the analysis of obligation, but nevertheless do not wish to pass them by without some comment.

Any full analysis of the notion of obligation to oneself depends upon the view of the self which underlies the explication. I am in general agreement with the analysis of the self presented by Mead, but even if the self is considered as primarily social, it does not seem to me that we can have an obligation to ourselves, or make commitments to ourselves, in the same sense as we have obligations or make commitments to others. An essential element of our ordinary notion of obligation is that once the commitment is made and the obligation incurred, it cannot be nullified or abrogated merely by having the person who made the commitment and has the obligation decide that he is no longer bound by it. But we can always do this with commitments and obligations to ourselves—we are bound by them only as long as we choose to be bound. Hence I am inclined to think that the phrase "obligation to oneself" is more metaphorical than literal.

We do say "You owe it to yourself," but often, I think, we mean by this not that one has an obligation to oneself, but rather that one does *not* have a supposed obligation to someone else, and therefore his own interests are relevant considerations in the situation. That is, "You owe it to yourself" often means that the conflict is one of interest, not of obligation.

One sense in which we may perhaps be said to have an obligation to ourselves is this: As a member of a community we may on occasion have an obligation to consider the interests of each of the members of the community who will be affected by some proposed action, and in this we also have an obligation to consider the interests of ourselves *as a member of the community.* This is one sort of obligation we do not often fail to fulfill and we are sometimes commended for neglecting. But in these cases the commitment made is not to oneself but to the community, and so is in accord with the analysis we have given.

I should like here also to allay the suspicion the reader may have that I have divorced obligation from evaluation absolutely. There is a sense in which our obligations rest upon considerations of value, but it is not the sense expounded in the usual teleological theory, and, I think, it can best be understood only after obligation and evaluation have been independently analyzed.

Thus far our analysis of obligation as resulting from the making of a commitment seems fairly straightforward, and though difficulties are admitted in particular, it may not be unduly rash to assert that we can, in general, empirically ascertain what commitments an individual has made and to whom. But a further qualification is yet to be explored. When any commitment is made, whether implicit or explicit, a number of exceptional conditions are usually either stated or implied—conditions that, if they occur, will nullify the commitment. Thus if I promise to attend a meeting or make a speech, it is understood that if I become ill, or a member of my immediate family is seriously ill, or I am called to serve on a jury or testify in a trial, or ..., I no longer have an obligation to attend the meeting or make the speech, although I may have an obligation to notify the persons concerned that the exceptional circumstance has intervened. Even such

a basic commitment as that of the citizen to aid in the defense of the
nation may be nullified or at least limited by certain exceptional conditions, such as the taking of certain religious vows. Hence, when we
assert that someone has an obligation, we are asserting not only that
a commitment has been made, but also that no exceptional conditions
prevail.

In general we are unable to list *all* the implied exceptional conditions
accompanying any commitment, but when particular circumstances
arise, we must decide whether or not they constitute an exception.
Some generally acknowledged exceptional conditions apply to almost
every commitment. If, for example, a commitment is extracted through
deceit or under false pretenses, or made only under coercion, then it
is not considered binding. Many commitments are made conditional
to the performance of some action by the claimant and are nullified if
this action is not performed. But since there often remain a number of
exceptional conditions we cannot specify antecedent to their occurrence, obligation must be considered a concept of the sort which H. L. A.
Hart has called *defeasible*.

Adapting the term from the language of legal discourse, Hart argues
that it may be applied to many utterances in ordinary language which
are similar in important respects to legal concepts. Legal utterances
can usually be opposed in two ways, Hart claims, by denial of the facts
on which they are based, or a plea that other facts present bring the
case under some recognized head of exception. Hence, it is not usually
possible to specify necessary and sufficient conditions for the application of a legal concept, for such concepts can only be explained with
the aid of a list of exceptions showing when they may not be applied.
Those concepts for which conditions may be specified but which do
not apply if one or more of a number of different contingencies hold
are what Hart calls "defeasible concepts."[10] It appears from our discussion that obligation is a concept of this sort. This should not be at
all surprising, since "obligation" is a legal as well as a moral term.

There are, then, cases in which we will literally be unable to say
finally whether or not someone has a particular obligation, since circumstances may arise for which there is no precedent for a decision
as to whether or not they constitute an exceptional condition. But a
great many situations remain in which we can quite confidently say
there are no exceptional conditions or, conversely, some condition does
constitute an exception, and, consequently, we may assert with a high

[10] "The Ascription of Responsibility and Rights," *Proceedings of the Aristotelian
Society*, LIX (1948–1949), 172–175.

degree of probability that some person has an obligation to perform some action.

This, then, completes the outline of an empirical theory of obligation. Claims are validated by the making of commitments. We cannot move directly from commitment to obligation; even though a commitment is made, the obligation depends upon the existence of a claimant.

Once a commitment is made and a rightful claimant exists, an obligation holds until it is either fulfilled or abrogated. An obligation may be abrogated by any one of several methods: the claimant can cancel an obligation by explicitly withdrawing his claim; the removal of the claimant, by death or otherwise, will nullify the obligation unless an alternate claimant is designated; or the obligation may be nullified by the occurrence of any of the several exceptional conditions. The abrogation of any particular obligation may leave the claimee free of any obligation to the claimant, or while removing one obligation it may impose another.

With this sketch of a theory of obligation as a background, we may now turn to the formal analysis of judgments of obligation.

A judgment of obligation is *grounded* when evidence is presented sufficient to establish that the person who is said to have the obligation has made a commitment, and the claim made is one covered by this commitment.

When the obligation ascribed arises from an explicit commitment, it is relatively simple to establish that the commitment was made. One needs only to show that the person in question has publicly performed one of the several acts employed in the community for the purpose of binding oneself to the performance of any action.

When an obligation arises from an implicit commitment, it must be shown that an explicit commitment was made and the content of the commitment and the circumstances under which it was made are such as to imply the further commitment, or that the claimee has himself made similar claims on other members of the community.

As we have noted, it is sometimes difficult to establish conclusively that an implicit commitment has been made. The way we may do this is by showing that within the given community an explicit commitment of type X is generally taken to imply a commitment of type Y, as in our society a commitment to return a borrowed object is generally taken to imply a commitment to return it in the same condition as when borrowed.

We have here another indication of the ubiquity of the notion of community and its importance in moral problems. No judgment of obligation can be understood without reference to some particular community. Even with obligations arising from an explicit commitment made by one individual to another, the commitment must be made by use of one of the recognized act forms of a community and the interpretation of the specific content of the commitment is most often determined in accord with standard practice in that community. Thus difficulty sometimes arises over commitments made by one community to another, or by a member of one community to a member of another, reaching its height in international affairs. Each of the parties involved interprets the commitment in accord with the standard practice of his own community and hence may have different expectations about what will or ought$_0$ be done. This remark is not to be taken as critical of the practice of making intercommunity commitments; only by the making of such commitments are larger communities formed.

When the obligation ascribed arises from a commitment entered into merely by membership in a community, the grounding of the judgment of obligation requires evidence that the claimee is a member of the community and the claim is one acknowledged as valid in the community. We usually assume, correctly, that the claimee is a member of the community and will respond as a member of the community; hence we often make no mention of this condition in our defense of a judgment. But even so, our ascriptions of obligation are often couched in terms making their relativity to a community explicit. We say, for example, "As a father, you have an obligation to provide for the education of your child," or "If you are an American, it is your duty to help defend the country."

This condition is generally not difficult to fulfill when the reference made is to actual communities, but our ascriptions of obligation often have reference to ideal communities as well—most often to the ideal community of man. All that we can justifiably do in this regard is to assert what an agent's obligation *would be* if the ideal community were actual and address the agent as a potential member of a potential community whose acceptance of this obligation is a step in the process of transforming the ideal community into an actual one. If the agent does regard himself as a member of this community, his obligation may be as real as any other; but if the agent refuses to consider himself a member of the ideal community, we can only urge that he ought$_e$ do so.

Once we have assumed or proven the membership of the claimee in the community, the judgment is grounded by showing that a law or regulative principle accepted in the community applies to the situation, or the particular act is one that furthers the pursuit of community goals.

The *felt normative force* of judgments of obligation, like judgments of evaluation, has several sources, including the dynamic or emotive character of the language, the effect of the ceremonial aspect of ethical discourse, and the status and authority of the speaker. But far more important than these is the authority given the statement by the agent's having freely committed himself. With regard to obligation, it is as Kant said: We give ourselves the moral law, and only when and as we give it to ourselves is it binding on us. When I make an explicit commitment, I bind myself to the performance of some act. The judgment of obligation merely asserts that I am so bound. I feel it as authoritative because it is myself who am the source of its authority. Similarly, as a member of a community, even when I am the object of its laws or moral rules I am also a participant, however remote, in the formulation and promulgation of these rules; and so to the degree in which my self is involved in the life of the community, I am myself the source of authority.

The normative force of judgments of evaluation was found to be, in many instances, a force of attraction rather than of compulsion. The force of judgments of obligation is, on the contrary, a compulsive force; we feel *compelled* to fulfill our obligations even when we have no desire to do so. But the compulsion of obligation is not externally imposed, rather it stems from our own volition. A judgment of obligation is essentially different from a command, with which some philosophers have sought to identify it, in that it does not represent an imposition of the will of the speaker on the agent, but rather seeks to achieve its aim, the performance of an action by the agent, by making the agent aware of his own will as expressed in the commitments he has made. I am not claiming that the language of obligation is never used by one who seeks to impose his will on another, for it obviously is. But my position is that wherever the *only* reason for asserting an action to be obligatory is that the speaker wants it done, the judgment is not warranted.

The role of volition in ethics is most pronounced in its connection with obligation. But even here I cannot agree with those who take ethical judgments, or even judgments of obligation, to be expressions of a volitional decision made by the speaker. Volition is involved, but it has been assigned to the wrong party.

The important volition is not that of the speaker, but that of the person said to have the obligation. The making of a commitment is usually an act of volition—always in explicit commitments, often in others. For example, often our entrance into membership in a community is a volitional act—we decide to get married and thereby create a new community with all the commitments involved, or we decide to go to a particular college, or join a fraternity or a political party, or migrate to a new nation, or even to remain where we are. All these volitional acts result in commitments and obligations, but once these volitional decisions are made, no further volition is necessary for the assertion of a judgment of obligation—except, of course, for the volitions required in any speech act.

Our tendency to feel bound by commitments we have made, to feel as authoritative judgments of obligation referring to these commitments, results, of course, from the conditioning we receive from early childhood, with rewards and punishments being meted out as we do or do not honor our commitments. It is probably true that in a community in which promises were never kept, the members would feel no force in judgments of obligation, except as these were externally imposed and enforced. But it is equally true that there could be no such community, or if there were it would be short-lived. For the continuing existence of a community as a community depends upon the members being able to rely on each other to fulfill their commitments, obey the laws, keep agreements and promises, work for the common good. Just as the existence of the community is a basis for obligations, so obligations are the mortar of the community, cementing the members together in a functional whole.

A grounded judgment of obligation is justified or *warranted* when it is shown that no exceptional conditions prevail.

I have already remarked on the difficulties of determining, in some instances, what constitutes an exceptional condition. Since we can only infrequently know for sure what conditions would be exceptional, it is generally true that the more we know about all of the existing circumstances, the higher the probability that we have overlooked no exceptional condition. Hence the importance, for judgments of obligation as for judgments of evaluation, of getting all the available facts and basing our judgments on the widest possible knowledge of the situation.

When a judgment of obligation has been grounded and it has been established that there are no exceptional conditions, the judgment is warranted in the only way we have of warranting such judgments without abandoning empiricism. If someone still asks "But ought I really?" we must either take this as an indication that he accepts the possibility of some superempirical proof, or we must construe his question as one not about obligation but about evaluation—as "But ought$_e$ I really?" The ambiguity that prevails throughout ethical discourse between value and obligation is markedly present here. If one asks "Why ought$_o$ I do X?" and is truthfully answered "Because you promised," unless he can cite some prevailing exceptional condition, the questioner can pursue the argument only by asking, "But why ought I keep my promises?" But this question is only significant if the "ought" is taken to be "ought$_e$." If it is meant as "ought$_o$," then it must be that the speaker does not understand the meaning of "promise"; it is tautological that anyone making a promise has an obligation to keep it.

This point is clear if we consider the statement "I promise to do X, but I have no obligation to do it." Given our usual tendency to construe all utterances as significant if possible, we would probably understand this as "I am assuming an obligation to do X, but I had no prior obligation to assume it," as perhaps when a man assumes the debts of a dead brother. If, however, we take the statement as "I promise to do X, but, having promised, I have no obligation to fulfill my promise," our ordinary reaction is: "Then you haven't promised." The statement is a contradiction; a promise just *is* an act devised for the purpose of instituting an obligation.

Therefore, if a significant question is to be asked, it must be "Why ought$_e$ I keep my promise?"—"Why would it be better if I kept my promises?" This is indeed a real question, often requiring an answer, and shall be considered in the next chapter. But I may say now, that however it is answered, the answer usually has no effect on the truth or falsity of the asserted judgment of obligation, "You ought$_o$ really." The point to be made here is that when this question is asked, the discussion is shifted from obligation to evaluation.

It may have been noted that throughout this analysis of judgments of obligation I have had no occasion to take into account the inclinations and desires of the agent at the time he is said to have an obligation. *Once a commitment is made,* obligation and inclination are, in general, quite independent.[11] One may have obligations to do things he is feverishly anxious to do, or things he is feverishly anxious to avoid doing. If we do not so often speak of actions we wish to perform as obligatory, it is not because they are not obligatory, but because, desiring to do them, we do not need the added motivational force of a judgment of obligation to incite us to act. It is when inclination is opposed to obligation that one is moved to ask in response to a warranted judg-

---

[11] There are instances in which the desires and inclinations of the agent enter into the expressed and implied exceptional conditions. Here, of course, obligation and inclination are no longer independent.

ment of obligation, "But ought I really?" Here the "ought" is "ought$_e$."—the questioner asking for some reason for acting *other than* the reason that he has an obligation.

In this and the preceding chapter I have proposed analyses of the two fundamental types of ethical judgment, judgments of evaluation and judgments of obligation. In both analyses I have attempted to adhere closely to our common sense notions and ordinary usage of ethical terms while avoiding any reference to or dependence upon non-empirical concepts or synthetic a priori statements. My desire to remain empirical has meant that the analyses accord only with a portion of common usage, for, admittedly, actual ethical discourse contains many references to religious or metaphysical authority, "self-evident" principles, and the dictates of intuition and conscience. Insofar as it contains these aspects we must, as empiricists, hold that common usage is mistaken, that any ethical judgment based on nonempirical concepts is for that reason unwarranted.

One of the purposes of this analysis has been to demonstrate that nonempirical concepts are not necessary for ethics. I have not taken the course of simply ruling them out because they are nonempirical, thus leaving ethics impoverished. Rather I have tried to show that an empiricist ethics can be constructed to cover the whole range of ethical experience—in accordance in large measure with common usage and not outrageous to common sense. Judgments of evaluation are empirical insofar as they refer finally to goods and evils directly realized in immediate experience, as the great majority of our ordinary value statements do. Judgments of obligation are empirical insofar as they refer to commitments actually made by persons or entailed in community living, as the great majority of our ordinary obligation statements do. We have no sense organs with which we can "see" an obligation, any more than we can "see" fatherhood, but a man may have an obligation as truly as he can be a father. We may observe the actions which obligate a man as easily as we can those which make him a father—in fact, more easily, since the latter actions are not often publicly performed, whereas the former almost always are.

My analyses do not pretend to be complete, but even so they have become quite complex. It has been necessary not only to distinguish two fundamentally different types of ethical judgment, but also to treat separately several subtypes of each—subtypes that are grounded and warranted in somewhat different ways and may have different sources of normative force.

One result of this complexity is to limit seriously the number of general statements we can justifiably make about ethical discourse. We cannot claim to be able to empirically justify *all* ethical judgments, nor can we even claim this is in principle possible. But this cannot be taken as justifying the counter assertion that, in general, ethical judgments are nonempirical, or that all ethical judgments are in principle incapable of empirical warrant. The great majority of ethical judgments are open to empirical justification, and in a great many instances we have enough evidence available to allow us to make statements about what is good or bad, what ought or ought not to be done, confident that our assertions have a high degree of probability. We must be content to admit that though most ethical judgments are empirical, some may not be finally justifiable.

Similarly, we can make no general statements about the relation of emotions, feelings, desires, inclinations, or volitions to ethical judgments, nor assert that a knowledge of consequences is either essential or nonessential to the justification of such judgments. Sometimes emotions and volitions are of central importance, at other times they are negligible; in some instances a knowledge of consequences is essential, in others not. Most often, the more knowledge we have about the situation the better, but this does not mean the range of facts relevant to any ethical judgment is unlimited, as only a few facts, or facts of a particular kind, may be pertinent.

Such results may seem very messy and quite unacceptable to many who demand elegance and simplicity in ethical theory, or seek a comprehensive view expressible in a few generalizations applicable to all ethical discourse, or demand the precision of the formalized language of physics in any statement to be admitted as empirical. But the language of ethics does not differ from the language of science in being nonempirical; rather, it differs in being ordinary language, the language of common sense and every day conversation with its emotive and motivational significance, its vagueness and ambiguity, trailing off at the edges into metaphor, into metaphysics, religion, and a dependence upon good will or a "moral sense" or "wisdom" to make decisions when the available facts are not sufficient to dictate a rational choice. I suspect that if philosophers would take a careful look at the language of science as it is actually used, they would find it not so different from this. My excuse for the complexity the proposed analysis allows is that ethical discourse happens to be this way. Insofar as any analysis offers much more elegance and much greater simplicity, it will be, I think, inadequate and misleading.

Another result of the complexity of this analysis also accords with our common experience, but may be unwelcome to some theorists. This is the degree and variety of conflict allowed. Given our analysis with its several levels of value and obligation and the acknowledged relativity of both judgments of evaluation and judgments of obligation to particular communities, we may have conflicts not only between value and obligation but also between values and between obligations. And, I submit, this is in fact the ethical situation as experienced. Hence, no matter how correct an analysis of evaluation or obligation may be, it will remain incomplete as long as it fails to consider these conflicts. In the next and final chapter I shall consider the problems raised by these conflicts and, in general, the relation of value to obligation.

CHAPTER VI

CONFLICTS AND RELATIONSHIPS

IN THE WORLD of common sense the question of whether there are such things as values and obligations no more presents a real problem than does the question of the existence of the external world. In almost any context in which humans find themselves, we take for granted that some things are better than others, some actions will have better results than others, and that we have obligations to perform some actions and to refrain from performing others. But although the existence of values and obligations in general is seldom questioned, we are often at a loss to know in a given situation just what particular course of action we should undertake. And this difficulty does not always stem from an inability to distinguish good from evil, or from lack of knowledge of what sorts of acts are obligatory. It stems, rather, from the fact that in many situations we find a multiplicity of values, not all of which can be realized, and a multiplicity of obligations, not all of which can be fulfilled.

If nothing else, the foregoing analyses of evaluation and obligation accord with this experienced complexity of human affairs. These analyses admit a plurality of ethical judgments and a variety of possible conflicts, and hence make plausible the large number of ethical disagreements that do occur.

Many of these disagreements are over what, in a given situation, actually is good for some individual or group or what obligations an individual or community may actually have. Insofar as ethical disagreements are of this sort, our analyses provide a framework for settling them. If one disputant asserts that B has an obligation to perform act X and the other asserts that B has no such obligation, the two assertions are, in accord with our analysis, logically contradictory and only one of them may be a warranted judgment of obligation. The analysis has shown that in some such situations, though perhaps not in all, it is possible to determine empirically which of the opposed judgments is justified. Or if the assertions are "X is good for A (or group A)" and "X is not good for A (or group A)," these also are logically contradictory and only one may be a warranted judgment of evaluation. Here, too, it is possible to determine empirically the one justified. Great practical difficulty may be encountered in amassing evidence enough to allow for justification of one judgment or refutation of the other, but this is true of disagreements of any sort and not merely of ethical ones.

But though our analysis does provide methods for the rational resolution of this class of disagreements, a great many remaining disputes
fall outside this class. These disputes arise from conflicts of values or
obligations. For, though "X is good for group A" and "X is not good
for group A" are contradictory and cannot both be warranted judgments, "X is good for group A" and "X is not good for group B" are
not contradictory and may both be warranted. And if an individual is
a member of both groups A and B, our analysis, so far, would be of
little help to him in deciding on the proper course of action. Hence we
must yet consider what can be said about the resolution of such conflicts. It may not be amiss to repeat here that what can or cannot be
done with regard to these conflicts in no way alters the status of the
conflicting judgments of evaluation or obligation as empirically warranted.

In the analyses I have offered, value and obligation have been presented as independent. I have insisted that we have no obligation to
perform acts productive of good merely because they are productive
of good, and have been able to offer no assurances that obligatory actions will always result in good. In many situations we can tell what
our obligations are only by first ascertaining what actions would be
most conducive to the good of some community; but the source of the
obligation here is not the goodness to be produced, rather it is the commitment we have made to the community. Likewise, we cannot determine what would be good for an individual or group in any situation
without taking into account the obligations he or they have. Here the
goodness is not implied by the obligatory character of some actions;
rather it is related to the predictable consequences of fulfilling or failing to fulfill these obligations.

But if value and obligation are independent in that neither implies
the other and neither is reducible to the other, they are also integrally
related in that in almost every context a persistent inquiry into one
will lead to consideration of the other and in most cases we seek to
settle conflicts of one by appeal to the other. The remainder of this
chapter will be largely an expansion of this remark. The discussion
will be largely schematic and does not pretend to offer final answers to
any of the major problems presented, but perhaps it will at least plot
pathways that may prove fruitful if further explored.

Given the analyses of the preceding chapters, in any occurring
human situation several classes of *warranted* ethical judgments are
possible: (*a*) judgments of evaluation asserting what is or would be

best for each of the persons directly implicated in the situation, considered merely as individuals; (*b*) a judgment of evaluation asserting what is best for all of the persons directly implicated, considered as a group; (*c*) judgments of evaluation asserting what is best for each of the communities of which the individuals involved are members; (*d*) judgments of obligation asserting that the individuals involved have obligations to each other; (*e*) judgments of obligation asserting that the individuals involved have obligations to others who are not directly implicated in the situation; (*f*) judgments of obligation asserting that the individuals have obligations to communities of which they are members.

Conflicts may arise between judgments of any of the different classes or between judgments of the same class. Fortunately, we are not often faced with situations in which all the possible sources of conflict are actualized. Usually what is best for an individual coincides with what is best for some of the communities of which he is a member, and his obligations to these communities are, perhaps more often than not, in harmony with what is best for the community. And most often, the individuals involved share membership in one or more communities and hence have values and obligations in common. But even so, the actual conflicts are often more than we are prepared to cope with.

If we accept the independence of value and obligation, three types of conflict are possible: (1) There are conflicts between values. What is good for one individual may be bad for another; what is good for one community may be bad for another; what is good for an individual may be bad for a community; and vice versa. (2) There are conflicts between obligations. A person may have an obligation to perform act X and an obligation to perform act Y, in a context in which it is impossible to do both. Or different persons or groups may have obligations to perform actions that bring them into conflict. (3) There are conflicts between value and obligation. Someone may find an action to be conducive to his good and yet be an action he has an obligation not to perform, or an obligatory act may be conducive to evil. It is possible, too, to have a situation involving all three types of conflict; one may, for example, have to choose between two actions, both obligatory and both leading to good, but mutually exclusive.

This variety and number of potential conflicts serves to emphasize again the misleading ambiguity of our ordinary ethical language. If someone asserts "*A* ought to do *X*" and is answered "*A* ought not do *X*," we cannot tell merely from these statements whether the conflict is one of evaluation or obligation, or even if the statements are logically incompatible. Nor will our device of adding subscripts "o" and "e" to "ought" help much. Before we can see clearly what the conflict is, let alone resolve it, we must expand the statements to make their content explicit. The expanded statements may be of the form "It would be better for A if X were done" and "It would be better for A if X were not done," or "A has an obligation to do X" and "A does not have any obligation to do X"; if so, the statements are logically incompatible. Or the statements, when expanded, may be of the form "A has an obligation to do X" and "It would not be better for A if X were done," or "It would be better for group B if X were done" and "It would not be better for group C if X were done." In these instances both statements of either pair may be warranted and the statements are not logically opposed. Perhaps the frequency of disputes of the latter sort, carried on without the full expansion ever being made, has led some philosophers to assert that conflicting ethical judgments are never logically opposed and hence cannot be empirical statements, but merely express conflicting attitudes or emotions. Our analysis exposes the error of this assertion and also shows how it is plausible that the error should have been made. Further it provides a method for making clear the logical relations between the conflicting ethical judgments.

In order to determine the locus and nature of the conflict, it is generally necessary to expand each of the conflicting statements so as to indicate whether the judgment is of evaluation or of obligation. If a judgment of evaluation, the expansion must be extended to specify the person or group for whom the object, action, or state of affairs is asserted to be good or bad. If a judgment of obligation, the expansion must specify to whom the agent is obliged, who has a valid claim.

When the expansion is made we may see that even such apparently incompatible statements as "A has an obligation to do X" and "A has an obligation not to do X" need not be logically opposed and both may be warranted. For the expanded statements may be "A has an obligation to C to do X" and "A has an obligation to D not to do X."[1] These are not contradictory but are conflicting judgments. When we speak of conflicting ethical judgments, we may mean either that the judgments are logically incompatible or, although they are logically compatible, the judgments direct or recommend actions that are not compatible.

---

[1] The reader may feel impelled to protest that A cannot have an obligation to both do and not do X, for this is impossible and we cannot have an obligation to perform the impossible. I agree, but the fact is not that A has an obligation to both do and not do X. Rather he has an obligation to do X and he has an obligation not to do X. Or, if these are to be combined, he has obligations to both do and not do X. It is impossible that he fulfill both of these obligations, but it is by no means impossible that he have them.

The judgments of evaluation and obligation discussed in the foregoing analyses may be called *first-level* ethical judgments. The question to be faced now is this: Given that these first-level ethical judgments are generally open to empirical justification, are there also empirically justifiable *second-level* judgments, judgments that mediate between conflicting first-level judgments? Or must we admit that second-level judgments are only emotive or volitional; consequently, although we have empirical methods of deciding what is best for persons or groups and what actions are obligatory for an individual, we have no rational method of settling conflicts of values or obligations?

My answer, the only answer I believe an empiricist justifiably able to give, is that, in general, second-level ethical judgments can be empirically warranted, but *there is no empirical method of assuring that these judgments will then be accepted as authoritative directives.*

Many contemporary philosophers seem to have confused the question "Can ethical judgments be empirically justified?" with the question "Are empirical methods sufficient to resolve all ethical disagreements?" And they so construe this latter question that it may be answered affirmatively only if it can be shown that in every situation of conflict it is possible to empirically ascertain *one* course of action to be *the* right act, and that all empiricists, merely in consequence of their empiricism, must accept this as the right act or be guilty of some error of reasoning. It is my belief that the two questions are quite distinct and, once the full content of ethical judgments is made explicit, it may be seen that an affirmative answer to the first does not entail an affirmative answer to the second.

The facts as I see them are: Though second-level judgments are capable of empirical justification, the acceptance of them as a basis for the resolution of ethical conflicts depends also upon what we ordinarily call the "good will" or "moral sense" of the disputants. This conclusion may be somewhat disappointing to those who like to talk of a "scientific ethics," and may be hailed as an indication of the fatal weakness of empiricism by those who would have us turn instead to the spurious certainty of metaphysical or religious theories. Whether either reaction is justified I leave to the reader to decide after the analysis has been completed. But if we are to adhere to our intention of presenting a defensible empirical ethical theory, it is essential we not only spell out in detail what the empiricist can justifiably say in ethical situations, but also admit freely what it is that he cannot say.

The basis of my contention that second-level judgments are capable of empirical warrant is that the terms "first-level" and "second-level" are relative terms referring to a difference in function rather than a difference in content. What are first-level judgments in one context may be second-level judgments in another. Hence second-level judgments are capable of being warranted by the methods set forth in the preceding chapters. The task that remains is to show how these judgments function in the various types of conflict.

Let us first consider conflicts of value. There are several different forms of such conflict—between individuals, between communities, and between individuals and communities—and for each form of conflict there is some kind of ethical judgment that functions as a second-level judgment to which we ordinarily appeal when we seek a rational resolution of the conflict. The second-level judgment may resolve the conflict either by directing a course of action different from that directed by either of the conflicting judgments, or by reinforcing one of the conflicting judgments. If the former, the second-level judgment is usually a judgment of evaluation asserting some action to be best for a larger group than that to which either of the conflicting judgments refer; if the latter, the second-level judgment may be either a judgment of evaluation of this sort or a judgment of obligation.

Conflicts of value arise between two *individuals* A and B when there are warranted judgments of evaluation asserting that it would be best for A if X were done and best for B if X were not done, or asserting that it would be best for A if X were done and best for B if Y were done, in a context in which both X and Y cannot be done. Here several second-level judgments are possible, depending in part on the relationship of A to B. The second-level judgment may be a judgment of evaluation asserting that some course of action would be best for A and B, considered as a group; or if A and B share membership in some community the second-level judgment may assert some action to be best for the community. Or either A or B may have some obligation in the situation. Suppose A and B are students preparing for an examination and A has borrowed from B a book necessary for the preparation, promising to return it several days before the exam. It might then be true that it would be best for A if he kept the book and would be best for B if the book were returned. Hence we have a conflict of value. But here a third warranted judgment may serve as a second-level judgment in the conflict, that is, A has an obligation to return the book.

A second form of conflict is between an *individual* and a *community* of which the individual is a member. In this situation the second-level judgment is a judgment of obligation asserting that the individual ought, to do what is best for the community—as a member of the community he has an obligation to promote the welfare of the community. This is not to say that in every such case the individual must abandon his goals and adopt those of the community or conform to the dictates of the community. It may be, rather, that what is best for the community is the resignation of the individual from the community— if it is a community from which resignation is possible. Or it may be that what would be best for the community would be to alter its goals and adopt those proposed by the individual. This is the way in which communities progress. The task of the individual is to try to demonstrate to the community that it would indeed be best for the community to adopt the goal or course of action he proposes. But even if he fails to persuade the group and is forced to acquiesce by community pressure, it may still remain true that the community ought, to have acted differently.

Conflicts between *communities* may be either between exclusive communities, between overlapping communities, or between communities, one of which is included in the other.

In conflicts between the values of exclusive communities, the communities involved, though exclusive, may yet both be members of a larger community. A rational resolution of such conflicts may be based upon a second-level judgment stating what is best for the larger community, reinforced by a judgment of obligation to the effect that the members of the smaller communities, and perhaps the communities as communities, have obligations to promote the welfare of the larger community. Thus conflicts between civic groups are resolved by considering what is best for the city as a whole; conflicts between states by reference to what is best for the nation.

Conflicts between exclusive communities not both members of a larger community require the projection of an ideal community if we are to arrive at a warranted second-level judgment. This is the function played by the ideal of a community of all mankind in our efforts to attain a rational resolution of disputes between nations. Lacking an actual world community, our only method of resolving such conflicts, apart from purely partisan solutions, is by considering the conflicting nations as members of an ideal world community including them all, and then seeking to determine what would be best for this larger community.

Conflicts of value between nonexclusive communities always involve conflicts of obligation as well. The individual who is a member of both communities has obligations to each of them, and in terms of these a warranted second-level judgment may be reached. Hence I shall leave further examination of such conflicts to our later discussion of conflicts of obligation.

In this section I have attempted to indicate directions in which we may seek a rational settlement of conflicts of values. This everywhere involves the application of some second-level judgment that may then function directively in settling the conflict. These second-level judgments are justifiable in quite the same ways as are first-level judgments. But even where a warranted second-level judgment can be asserted— and we often do not have enough knowledge to do more than make an informed guess—one or both parties to the dispute may still refuse to accept the conclusion as an authoritative directive.

Second-level judgments, in almost all instances, state either that an action would be best for some community or that some person has some obligation. They will, in general, be accepted as authoritative directives only by those who consider themselves members of the cited community or who are motivated to perform actions they recognize as obligatory. The acceptance of empiricism or the scientific method as the only method of obtaining knowledge does not entail either that one is willing to consider himself a member of any particular community or that he feel compelled to fulfill his obligations.

I may admit as empirically warranted the judgment that it would be best for community B if X were done, but I shall feel no need to do X unless I consider myself a member of B. And I may admit as empirically warranted the judgment that I have an obligation to fulfill some promise I have made, but I shall not be motivated to fulfill it unless my character is such that I ordinarily feel compelled to fulfill my obligations. It is here that the notions of good will, moral sense, or sense of duty become relevant to the resolution of conflicts. The man of good will is one who thinks of himself as a member of communities rather than as an isolated individual competing with all others, and a man with a sense of duty is one who feels compelled to fulfill his obliga- tions. As far as I can see, the acceptance of empiricism as a method does not necessarily carry with it either good will or a sense of duty.

Humans are motivated to act by at least three sorts of considerations. One may be motivated to perform some act by the consideration that the act is in his own interest, that it is in the interest of some community of which he is a member, or that he has an obligation to so act. The belief that an action is in one's own interest is usually sufficient in itself to move one to action. But the beliefs that an action is in the interests of the community or is obligatory are often not sufficient in themselves and may be markedly insufficient when they are opposed by the belief that the action is not in one's own immediate interest. Thus we are often driven to seek reinforcement of these motives by arguing that the furthering of one's own interests is dependent upon furthering the interests of the community or upon one's fulfilling his obligations.

The hitch in this line of argument is that for the man of good will, or possessing a sense of duty, such arguments are not necessary, but it is for him that they are most likely to be true. For the person who acknowledges his attachment to the community, it may well be true that if he fails to perform some act beneficial to the community or if he fails to fulfill an obligation, his loss of self-respect, his concern for the community welfare, and his unhappiness at having forsaken the community will more than offset any material advantage he may gain. But this assertion will not hold for the individual who feels no attachment to any community, who rather seeks his own advantage at no matter whose expense; and once that phase of the argument is abandoned, it becomes extremely doubtful that it could be shown in every instance to be to the individual's own interest to act for the best interests of the community. In some situations it is obviously false, as when the individual is asked to sacrifice his life in defense of the community.

The situation is quite similar for the person who does consider himself a member of some community, but then refuses to admit that he is also a member of some larger inclusive community that may be the referent of a second-level ethical judgment. And where the second-level judgment refers to an ideal community, the argument is even more difficult to carry through. The acceptance of empiricism by the individual does not in such cases entail the acceptance of the second-level judgment as authoritative.

I suspect social scientists may be able to show that the conditions most conducive to a good life for any human include his being a fully integrated member of a number of communities rather than a predatory individualist. And it is becoming increasingly evident in the twentieth century that the welfare of any one community is affected by the welfare of others and, perhaps, the future welfare of all communities depends upon the transformation of the ideal community of man and and of nations into an actuality. To the degree these beliefs are demonstrably true, the number of real conflicts will be reduced; in many apparent conflicts, we may be able to show that what is actually best for the individual is best for the community, or what is actually best for a community is best for a larger community. And here an acceptance of empiricism may be reflected in more general agreement in ethical matters.

But even the proven truth of these general statements would not guarantee their application to every particular case. I am convinced there will continue to be real conflicts of value, and where there are real conflicts the good will of the participants will be required if a rational resolution is to be achieved.

Conflicts of obligation, like conflicts of value, occur in several forms. There may be conflicts between obligations to individuals, between obligations to communities, or between an obligation to an individual and an obligation to a community.

Apparent conflicts of obligation can often be resolved by reference to the exceptional conditions implied in one or the other commitment. Where these conditions do not exist, a resolution of the conflict may be effected by reference to a second-level judgment of evaluation. For, in general, when we have to choose between two actions, both obligatory, the only rational method of deciding is through a process of evaluation, determining which action would do more good. When faced with the problem of two mutually exclusive actions, both of which I ought$_o$ do, I can decide between them only in terms of which obligation I ought$_e$ fulfill. Here again is an instance in which there is an obligation to perform the better of two alternative actions, but again the obligation does not originate merely in the goodness to be produced.

Among the exceptional conditions often implied is the condition that the commitment will no longer be binding if it conflicts with certain other obligations we may have. This is as true of commitments to communities as of the commitments we make to individuals and is extremely important in enabling us to decide on the course of our conduct.

Among the various communities in which an individual may function as a member, some are always recognized as having a primary claim on his allegiance—as communities that by their nature require a greater degree of attachment than do the others. In view of this generally recognized difference in degree of attachment, we may speak of *primary* and *secondary* communities. In the contemporary western world the two sorts of community generally regarded as primary are the family and the nation; social, civic, educational, labor, or business groups, political parties, and many such others, have the status of secondary communities. In the context of ethical discourse the ideal community of man is also often treated as a primary community.

We cannot specify categorically which sorts of communities are primary and which secondary, since they have varied with time and place. In Greece the city-state was a primary community; religious groups later became primary; and in our time, in large areas of the world, the political party has become a primary community. The community recognized as primary most generally and for the longest period of time is probably the family, though the boundaries of the family have been drawn quite differently at different times and places.

In our commitments to the various communities to which we belong, it is generally understood that obligations to the secondary communities may be overridden by obligations to a primary community. That is, it is implied in our commitment to the secondary community that the commitment will no longer be binding should it conflict with the welfare of a primary community.

In the preceding section discussion of conflicts of value between non-exclusive communities was postponed on the plea that they might be resolved in terms of the obligations involved. We may now see how this resolution is effected in those cases in which the conflict is between the goals of a secondary and a primary community. The individual who is a member of both communities is committed to further the welfare of each, but in view of the implied exceptional conditions his dominant obligation is to the primary community. This is not to say that the individual is always obliged to act to secure the *present* goals of the primary community. Rather his obligation, which provides the content of the second-level judgment, is to seek what is *best* for the primary community; this may mean shifting the goals of the primary community so they accord with those of the secondary community.

Where some exceptional condition does not prevail, the resolution of conflicts of obligation requires a process of evaluation. In conflicts between obligations to individuals—as when one has an obligation to A to do X and an obligation to B to do something incompatible with doing X—the second-level judgment of evaluation may assert that one of the alternatives would be best for all of the individuals involved, considered as a group, or that one of the alternatives would be best for some community in which all of these individuals are members.

In a conflict between an obligation to individual A and an obligation to a community of which A is a member, the decisive consideration is that A himself has an obligation to promote the welfare of the community; hence, the action prescribed by the second-level judgment is the alternative that is best for the community. In conflicts between an obligation to A and an obligation to a community of which A is not a member, the agent may be guided by a warranted judgment of evaluation asserting one of the obligatory actions to be best for some larger group including both.

Conflicts between obligations to communities may be resolved in very similar fashion. Here, too, if there are no exceptional conditions, a judgment of evaluation may function as a mediating second-level judgment. If the conflict involves obligations to exclusive communities, the second-level judgment to be sought is what would be best for the group that includes both communities. If the conflicting communities are not both parts of some larger actual community, we must make reference to an ideal community.

Where there are conflicts of obligation between nonexclusive communities, the type of second-level judgment depends upon the nature and relationships of the communities. Where the conflict is between secondary communities, one of which contains the other, the avowed purpose of the smaller community may be to promote the welfare of the larger, so the individual's obligation to the larger community overrides his obligation to the smaller. Or a settlement may be made in terms of what is best for a primary community containing the two conflicting groups—as a dispute between a political party and some faction may be settled by reference to what is best for the nation. When the conflict is between a secondary and a primary community, the individual's obligation to the primary community is dominant, as we have seen. In conflicts between obligations to primary communities, between a family and a nation, for example, if there is also a conflict of evaluation, the only source to which we can turn for a second-level judgment is to the projected ideal community of man.

It develops then that in many conflicts the decisive factor is an obligation to the ideal community of man. And this, in fact, is the function for which our projection of this ideal community is designed. But since it is only an ideal community, we cannot assert categorically that someone has an obligation to this community, as we can assert that he has an obligation to family or nation. We may justifiably say only "If you consider yourself a member of the community of man, then your obligation is so–and–so." It is not that an obligation to an ideal community is only an ideal obligation; it may be a real obligation. But until the community *functions* as a·community the obligation is real only for those persons who consider themselves members. It is for this reason that our second-level judgments referring to this ideal community are so often not accepted as a basis for resolving conflicts.

The task of justifying an assertion about what would be best for the community of man is, of course, no easy one. But this is not because the assertion is not empirical, rather because it requires much more empirical knowledge than we are able to have at the time it is needed.

Yet, even so, in many instances our knowledge of human nature and of the effects of certain situations on the humans involved allows us to assert with confidence statements about what is good or bad for mankind as a whole. I should think, for example, that there would be little doubt that the welfare of the community of man is not promoted by the development of situations in which children are required to be informers, reporting on the political deviations of their parents.

I have here argued that in most conflicts of obligation the individual faced with two or more obligations, only one of which he can fulfill, can make a reasoned choice between them in terms of a warranted second-level ethical judgment. It may be worth repeating here that the existence of a warranted second-level judgment usually only allows one to choose between obligatory acts; it does not do away with any of the existing obligations. The agent who performs the chosen act will usually still have some obligation to fulfill, though this may be different from the original one. For example, should I owe money to two persons and be able to repay only one at the promised time, I may be able to determine that it would be better to repay A than B, and do so, but I should still have an obligation to repay B also, as soon as I was able.

Intuitionists in ethics have often held that we choose between conflicting obligations by somehow seeing that one obligation is stronger than another, but the nature of the process of vision has remained quite obscure. I am willing to agree that we sometimes do "see" that one obligation outweighs another, but no inexplicable sort of intuition need be at work. The present analysis is at least a beginning in specifying what it is that can be "seen." Certain factors are relevant to a choice between obligatory actions: we must first ask, "Are there any exceptional conditions present in the situation?" These may be conditions either explicitly stated or implied in the commitment made, including the generally understood condition that an individual's cardinal commitment is to the primary communities. If no exceptional conditions exist, we must ask, "Which of the obligatory actions will have the best consequences?" One aspect of the relationship between value and obligation is presented here. Obligations do not arise simply from the good results an act may have, but where existing obligations actually conflict, we have no way of choosing between them except in terms of which would be more productive of good.

The one form of conflict not yet discussed is that between value and obligation. Conflicts may occur either between duty and interest, that is, between an obligation and the advantage of the person who has the obligation, or between an obligation and an action good for some person or group other than the person having the obligation.

In conflicts of the first sort, between an obligation I may have and *my* interest, it is again possible that the conflict be resolved by reference to exceptional conditions. Many of our commitments carry the implied stipulation that the commitment shall not be binding if it should prove harmful to the agent. If I promise to attend some social affair, for example, and conditions develop making it dangerous to fulfill the claim—a bad storm creating hazardous highway conditions, say—then the obligation ceases to hold. But the effects of the obligatory act on the agent's own interests are understood to be specifically *excluded* from the list of exceptional conditions in many of our explicit commitments and most of our commitments to communities. Hence, when we are concerned with these situations as presenting an ethical problem, it seems clear that our obligation overrides any consideration of our own interest. If any reinforcement of the judgment of obligation is necessary, as it often is, a second-level judgment generally applicable to such contexts is that the welfare of any community is generally furthered by the honoring of obligations and impaired by the breaking of them.

Conflicts between a judgment of obligation and a judgment of evaluation asserting something to be good for some person or community other than the agent either resolve into conflicts of obligation or are not felt as conflicts by the agent. If the agent is a member of the community to which the judgment of evaluation refers, he will have an obligation to this community. If he is not a member of this community, even though the judgments may direct incompatible actions, the conflict between them does not involve the agent. His only involvement in the situation is one of having an obligation, and unless he considers himself a member of the community he will not feel the situation as one of conflict.

The analyses presented of judgments of evaluation and judgments of obligation have allowed for a plurality of warranted ethical judgments in any given situation, and it has perhaps seemed objectionable in that it allows also for a plurality of real conflicts. But this plurality of ethical judgments not only allows real conflicts—and in this conforms to our experience—it also provides a way of resolving these conflicts. Where there are conflicting warranted ethical judgments, there is also possible a warranted second-level judgment which may serve as a basis for resolution of the conflict.

Philosophers have often seemed to take the position that empiricism in ethical theory could be seriously defended only if the empiricist could show that in every instance his methods could provide *one* warranted assertion as to what *ought* to be done—one assertion necessarily acceptable to every empiricist. But, as we have seen, this often cannot be done. Instead, there are often several warranted judgments, some of which may conflict. If they conflict, the empiricist's only method is to seek some other warranted judgment that mediates between the conflicting ones. But whether the conflict is actually resolved in terms directed by the second-level judgment depends upon the good will of the disputants and their desire to achieve a rational settlement. If someone insists on acting only for his own immediate interests, or only for the immediate interests of his community, that he is an empiricist in no way guarantees that he and other empiricists will be able to agree on all ethical problems. As we have remarked, a rational resolution of ethical disagreements is possible whenever all the disputants desire a rational settlement. And here good will is as important as a willingness to accept empirical evidence as the only source of knowledge.

If empiricism cannot assure agreement among empiricists, it can much less do so among those who think knowledge can be acquired by other than empirical methods. Persons or nations whose actions are founded upon dogma are not apt to be convinced by empirical arguments, whether their dogma is that of revelation, the destiny of the race, or the inevitable triumph of the proletariat. When dealing with such persons we may, as Stevenson argues, have finally to resort to some nonrational means of persuasion if they are going to be induced to act as we think they ought. But this necessity in no way alters the status of our ethical judgments as warranted assertions, any more than does the refusal of a religious group to accept the theory of evolution in any way alter the empirical status of the theory.

We may have reliable knowledge of the commitments persons have made. And we may have knowledge of the probable consequences of actions as they tend to increase or diminish satisfactions actually had by humans, and add to or subtract from the possibility of a good life for these humans. When our ethical judgments are based upon such knowledge, they will be empirically warranted assertions. They will be fallible, to be sure, and often unavoidably rest upon far less knowledge than we should like to have; nevertheless they remain the most reliable guides we can have in the often precarious pursuit of happiness. The sometimes-tragical difference between the empirically verified statements of a science and empirically warranted ethical judgments is that the consequences implicit in the scientific statement may occur whether or not anyone accepts the statement as true, while the goods predicted in the ethical judgment will accrue only if purposive human action is undertaken to bring them about.

This discussion of the various forms of ethical conflict and methods of rational resolution has revealed two types of ethical judgment combining the two functions of attributing value and ascribing obligation. One of these occurs in contexts of conflicting judgments of obligation. If it is true that I ought$_o$ do X and also ought$_o$ do Y, but cannot do both, then I may be able to resolve the conflict by ascertaining that I ought$_e$ do X. But when I then say, "Yes, I really *ought* to do X," or "X is the *right* thing to do," this statement is neither simply a judgment of obligation nor simply a judgment of evaluation. Rather, it asserts that I have an obligation to do X and X is the obligatory act most worthy of being done.

The second type of judgment combining the two functions occurs when actions judged to be conductive to the welfare of, or in the best interests of, some community are then asserted to be obligatory for some members of that community. The judgment of evaluation "It would be best for the community if X were done" combines with the judgment of obligation "As a member of the community I have an obligation to promote the welfare of the community" in the assertion, again, "Yes, I really *ought* to do X." If we want to distinguish this more complex "ought" from the others we may write it "ought$_{oe}$."

Since these statements combine a judgment of evaluation and a judgment of obligation, the task of providing a warrant for them is correspondingly complex, requiring that both the judgment of evaluation and the judgment of obligation be justified. If either of these proves unwarranted, the judgment itself is not warranted. This perhaps accounts for the strange structure of many ethical disputes, in which the argument shifts back and forth between questions of value and those of obligation without the relationship between them ever becoming clear.

Judgments asserting that an action is in the interest of some community and thus obligatory for some members of the community are very common in ethical discourse, but their complexity remains unnoticed because we habitually converse only with other members of our own community and thus speak as though all that is necessary to prove an act ought$_{oe}$ be done is to show that it is productive of good. Many of our ethical disagreements thus become disputes over which action really is best, with all the disputants tacitly agreeing that whichever act is best will be obligatory. The complex relation between value and obligation becomes obscured when all the disputants share in a commitment to a community which, because it is shared, needs not enter explicitly into the dispute.

It is only when we become involved in problems concerning members of communities other than our own that the full complexity of ethical problems becomes apparent and we come to realize that everyone need not admit as obligatory, or even as good, acts that have seemed obviously so to us. Some of us then go to the extreme of arguing that all evaluations are relative in some sense of this term which excludes their also being objective, and all obligations are illusory since these depend for their being on the objective existence of values. But this extremism is unnecessary. If we but abandon the indefensible notion that actions productive of good must be, by that very fact, obligatory, and if we recognize that statements about what is good are all ellipses for statements about what is good *for* some person or group, then we may see that judgments of evaluation can be objective, although relative to persons or groups, and judgments of obligation can be equally objective, whether or not there are any objective values. And if we realize also that actions productive of good for some community are obligatory only for members of that community, we may be able to see also that we shall never get all men to agree on what they ought₀ₑ to do until they reach the stage of considering themselves all members of the same community.

Some further aspects of the relationship between value and obligation may be revealed by attending to a topic I have hitherto avoided. I have insisted obligations are related to commitments, and once a commitment is made and a valid claim put forth, someone has an obligation. But I have said nothing at all about problems concerned with the making of commitments.

Throughout this book I have been almost wholly concerned with the problems of the moral agent seeking to decide what course of action to pursue. The ethical judgments I have discussed are those related to these problems. But the problem of the moral agent is not always only that of determining what is valuable and what obligations he now has or how best to fulfill them, it is also sometimes that of deciding what further obligations to take upon himself. That is, he must ask himself not only, "What commitments have I made?" but also, and of equal importance, "What commitments shall I now make?"

We may, of course, make commitments arbitrarily and capriciously, for no other reason than we feel a momentary impulse and act on it. And we may also later regret the making of a commitment, whether it was made capriciously or not, and wonder why we did it and whether we are really bound by it. Many of our sorrows have their inception in commitments injudiciously made and only later understood.

The world of the child is one of promises thoughtlessly given and later loudly and thoughtlessly denied. An important part of the process of growing out of childhood into maturity consists in coming to realize that promises, and commitments of any sort, are not purely personal matters but rather perform the function of binding persons together; while a promise may be capriciously made, it cannot be capriciously disavowed without this affecting our relations with others. We come also to realize that there are sensible and foolish commitments, and if we understand fully what is involved in our commitments when we make them, we are less likely to regret having to live up to them later. We begin then seriously to ask, "What commitments shall I make?" instead of acting merely on impulse.

The sentences we utter or write when we make a commitment and bind ourselves to perform some action are not themselves empirical assertions, or are rarely so. They are performatory uses of language. When someone says "I assure you that I will be at the meeting Tuesday," we cannot reasonably ask if he has spoken a truth or a falsehood, though we may reasonably ask if it is true or false that he will be at the meeting Tuesday. His utterance does not state a fact; it institutes or affirms an obligation. But we may ask of any contemplated commitment "Ought this commitment be made?" and the answer to this question will be an empirical assertion. The commitment made will be sensible or foolish as it is or is not directed by the answer given.

Some of the commitments we make are themselves obligatory actions because we are bound by earlier commitments to make present ones. Here we can say, "I ought₀ make this commitment," but whether this commitment is a sensible one or not depends upon the nature of the earlier commitment.

Many more of our commitments are entailed by our attachment to a community and thus, in a sense, made for us. We do not often debate whether we should make them or not, but simply accept them as a regular part of communal living. If we seriously doubt the wisdom of making some of these commitments, we may try to convince the other members of the community that it would be better if some of its goals or regulative principles were changed. Or, failing in that, we may ask, "Ought I continue to be a member of this community?" But we are not free to accept or reject the particular commitments as we see fit, since we are held to them as long as we remain in the community.

The remainder of our commitments are those we can make or not as we choose, although often the choice is restricted by the absence of any real alternatives. In these situations we can ask, "Ought I make this commitment?" and then suit our actions to the answer. Basically all of our commitments relate to commitments of this sort, since the questions "Ought I become a member of this community?" and "Ought I continue to be a member?" are but different forms of the question "Ought I make this commitment to the other members of this community?" And all our subsequent commitments to the community are entailed by this one. Accordingly, any discussion of what sort of answer can be given to this fundamental question will throw light upon the foundations of obligation in general.

We do not often ask the question in the form "Ought I make this commitment?" Rather we ask whether we should embark on some course of action that includes the making of a commitment. We ask, "Should I borrow money to buy a house?" "Should I enlist in the Army?" "Ought I marry him?" "Shall we have a child?" "Should I join the union?" "Ought I take this job?" "Should I accept this invitation?" And when we attempt to answer these questions, the method we invariably employ is that of envisioning the consequences of the proposed action and comparing these consequences with the probable consequences of alternative acts. That is, we decide whether or not to make new commitments on the basis of a judgment of evaluation; we undertake actions that involve the making of new commitments if we believe they will be productive of good; we do not make the commitment if we believe the consequences will be bad.

This is true also of those commitments apparently offering no real alternatives. There are always alternatives, but in these instances they are so much worse than the making of the commitment that we do not even seriously consider them as alternatives. It is perhaps unnecessary to add that not only concern for our own personal welfare moves us to undertake new obligations, we are moved also by a concern for the good of communities to which we belong and of the individual members of these communities.

Whenever we are faced with a choice of making or not making a commitment, or making one commitment rather than another, we must, if we are empiricists and desirous of behaving rationally, be guided in our choice by consideration of the values involved. This is the only alternative to caprice or dogma. Hence it develops that value and obligation are related in a way we have not hitherto noticed. An awareness of values underlies every assumption of a new obligation. Our only method of justifying acceptance of a new responsibility is by showing that it is a part of a sequence of actions that will probably be productive of good.

Similarly, the commitments entailed by our membership in a community are required of us only because they are generally thought to promote the good of the community. We are committed to work for these goals and to accept the regulative principles generally accepted in the community, but both these goals and these principles are adhered to because they are believed to be conducive to the good of the community. When these beliefs are no longer held, the members of the community demand that the goals or principles be changed.

The pattern is everywhere the same: sensible commitments are those undertaken in virtue of knowledge of probable prospective goods; foolish commitments are those undertaken without any foresight of probable consequences.

The empiricist ethical theory outlined here appears, then, to tread a path between the warring camps of the deontological and teleological theories. I have insisted, with the deontologists, that obligation is independent of value in that we can sometimes know a person has an obligation to perform some act without having to know the probable consequences of the act. I have been more radical than the deontologists in arguing that we have no obligation to perform actions productive of good merely because they are productive of good. But I have also argued that all obligations, if they are not the result of dogma or caprice, originate in considerations of values, and we can defend the making of any commitment only by claiming it to be a necessary part of some pattern of behavior that will probably lead to good. The position I have taken is: Though we have no obligation to perform acts productive of good merely because they are productive of good, our only reason for incurring any obligation is that it is necessary if some foreseen good is to be attained.

The theory proposed, then, is deontological with regard to the justification of judgments of obligation, and, if you please, the meaning of "obligation," but it is teleological with regard to the origin of obligation. To say that I have an obligation says nothing about any values to be achieved, but if there were no values to be achieved, I should never take upon myself any obligations.

With this final examination of the relation of obligation to value our outline of an empirical ethical theory is completed. In conclusion I offer a summary of what has been said and an indication of what yet remains to be said.

In summary: In our common speech we recognize two fundamentally different functions performed by ethical judgments, the attribution of values and the ascribing of obligations. And we employ two correspondingly different types of ethical judgment, judgments of evaluation and judgments of obligation. I have argued that most empiricist ethical theories have erred in not seeing that these two types of judgment require separate analyses, and only when the two are clearly distinguished can a sound empirical theory be formulated. In an attempt to formulate such a theory, I have sought to find criteria of adequacy and then to provide analyses satisfying these criteria. My point of view has been that once the pervasive ambiguity of ordinary ethical discourse is unravelled, the empirical cognitive content of ethical judgments can be specified without any necessity for becoming entangled in the puzzles of locating and defining an exhaustive set of "ethical predicates," or bewailing the incommensurability of "normative" and "descriptive" uses.

The analyses offered have been as complex as our ethical experience requires. I have nowhere sought simplicity for simplicity's sake at the expense of clarity and comprehensiveness. Normative ethical judgments are not merely simple statements of fact, offered only for the purpose of giving information. But this does not prevent them from being warranted empirical assertions. Judgments of evaluation all assert that some object, action, or state of affairs is valuable or disvaluable for some specific person or group. Judgments of obligation all assert that someone has or has not an obligation to some person or group to perform some action of a kind that can be voluntarily performed by humans. If we are to provide an empirical warrant for any ethical judgment, it is essential that this full statement of the judgment be given.

Judgments of evaluation may be empirically warranted by reference to satisfactions and dissatisfactions actually experienced or predicted and the relation of these satisfactions and dissatisfactions to the goal of a whole of life which is good in the living of it. Judgments of obligation may be empirically warranted by reference to commitments made and claims put forth and the relation of the individual to communities. In neither instance do we have to go beyond the empirical evidence to establish the judgment as warranted. In both instances there may be several sources of the felt normative force of the judgment and a number of types of judgment that must be warranted by somewhat different methods.

I have not been able to guarantee the existence of one and only one empirically warranted ethical judgment in every human situation. The approach taken has instead been that of admitting a plurality of warranted judgments and admitting the fact confronting us in our actual experience, that there are often real conflicts of values and of obligations. This plurality of ethical judgments not only allows for conflicts, it also makes possible a rational resolution of them. For every conflict there is some warranted second-level ethical judgment that may serve as a basis for settlement. But whether the conflict will actually be resolved in terms of this judgment depends upon the persons in the conflict being men of good will, interested in reaching a rational solution of the problem.

The analyses here presented have been carried on, as philosophical analyses so often are, in terms of what is theoretically possible and what can, in principle, be done. The actualities of the human situation are often such that what is in principle possible is in practice far beyond our powers of achievement. The methods I have outlined for the warranting of ethical judgments and the resolution of ethical conflicts are, I think, those we generally employ when we endeavor to determine the path of rational conduct. And we must candidly admit our applications of these methods are often unsuccessful—we find we cannot determine which judgments are warranted and which are not with any degree of conclusiveness, and we must often resort to persuasion, or even force, in settling disputes and conflicts. Finding this so, we then despair of the efficacy of empirical methods in ethics.

But our failures are not due to the insufficiency of empiricism as a method. Sometimes they stem from the failure of others to accept empirical evidence as decisive; sometimes they are due to lack of good will; but perhaps most often they are caused by our inability to gather enough empirical evidence to establish which of several different ethical judgments is most probable. The difficulty is not that ethical judgments are nonempirical, but that they require more empirical knowledge than we usually have.

Hence, the conclusion of an empirical analysis of ethics is not, as Hans Reichenbach has urged, the recommendation that we must trust our own volitions and demand that everyone else follow them—and, perhaps inevitably, that we seek by any means at our disposal to impose them on others. It is rather the recommendation that we must gather as much knowledge as we can about man and the world he lives in, for it is only through this knowledge that we shall ever be able to arrive at warranted ethical judgments and to have volitions that we can demand others follow because they are based upon warranted judgments and not merely because they happen to be *our* volitions.

Even when we have amassed a great store of knowledge, this does not assure us of a unique solution of every ethical conflict. This circumstance, too, is a consequence of our empiricism. The empiricist must eye with suspicion any theory that pretends to offer a guaranteed solution to every problem; yet he must insist there are no problems in which reason has no application and in which a careful study of the facts is not necessary. If there are insoluble problems, empiricists must admit them, but this is not the end of the matter. The practical mission in ethics is not only to solve individual problems as they arise, but also, and in the long run perhaps of more importance, to study the situations in which problems occur with an eye to creating conditions that increase the opportunity for choices between competing goods and tend to eliminate situations that force a choice between necessary evils.

The analysis I have presented is proposed as an outline for an empirical ethical theory. It is only that; it is far from being a complete theory. My intention has not been to offer to empirical philosophers a definitive treatise on morals, but rather to induce them to reorient their thinking. I have sought to extricate them from what has to a large extent become a futile round of bickering over problems set for them by G. E. Moore and the traditional theories, and to bring them back to consideration of the fundamental ethical situation—the human moral agent seeking to act rationally in the midst of all the uncertainties and confusions of life—as a source for ethical theory. For it is from our experience in these fundamental ethical situations that an empirical theory must come, if it is to come at all. No dialectic of ambiguous criticisms countered by subtle distinctions will take the place of a careful examination of actual ethical problems and a patient analysis of the ways in which we actually react toward them.

All the ethical judgments I have discussed in the course of this work have been construed as judgments connected with the problems of the moral agent. In a phrase earlier employed, they are all concerned with primary ethical problems; they are judgments directing the choice of one action over another in contexts calling for action. I have nowhere sought to discuss those judgments taken as central by many contemporary theorists, that is, judgments which assign praise or blame for actions already performed and direct attitudes of approval or disapproval toward the performers of these actions. I have said nothing directly about the problems of the moral critic; hence a large area of moral discourse remains untouched by this analysis.

Any complete ethical theory must, of course, consider the problems of the critic as well as those of the agent and analyze the language of the critic along with that of the agent. And the critic's task is not only that of assessing the praiseworthiness of actions, it involves also the assessment of character. I have not undertaken any discussion of the critic's use of the terms "right" or "wrong," and have completely avoided mention of such phrases as "morally good" and "morally bad." I believe these are problems for analysis which must follow rather than precede an analysis of the problems and language of the moral agent, and it is this prior task I have tried to perform. Once we have settled upon an analysis of the language employed in the context of primary ethical problems, the rest should present no major difficulties.

When the gaps have been filled in the analysis presented and these neglected areas of ethical discourse have been fitted into the pattern of analysis, we may have, in a sense, a completed ethical theory. But this does not signify the end of the moral philosopher's problems. Some contemporary writers have held that the role of philosophy in ethics ends when an analysis of the forms of ethical judgments has been given, that is, when an ethical theory has been formulated. But I am not of this mind. In my view the formulation of an ethical theory is merely a preliminary to the assuming of the traditional role of the philosopher in ethics: the role of the wise man *doing* ethics rather than that of the analyst *talking about* it.

Among the many problems involved in the philosophical doing of ethics, as opposed to the construction of ethical theories, is that of analyzing and clarifying the aims men seek to achieve and the regulative principles men adopt as guides in their pursuit of these aims. This is an assignment which, if well done, might go far toward lessening our sorrows. Many of the world's troubles stem from the dogged pursuit of illusory or contradictory goals and the stubborn adherence to inconsistent or inadequate principles. Some further problems emphasized by the present analysis are those of examining the relation of the individual to the community and making clear the sorts of commitment required by membership in a community—a spelling out, as it were, of the requirements of community life—as well as further examination of the nature of communities in general and in particular.

But aside from tasks of this sort there remains the great and challenging problem that has always confronted the philosopher, that of taking his theory and his methods of analysis into the area of actual ethical problems, and of using these tools in an effort to help prevent the great catastrophes threatening us. The philosopher must face the particular problems of his day and seek to employ his talent and training to find solutions which may serve as guides for those who have not his clarity and breadth of vision.

Perhaps no one will listen! But at least he will have done what he ought.

INDEX